The Economics and Science of Measurement

Metrology is the study of measurement science. Although classical economists have emphasized the importance of measurement *per se*, the majority of economics-based writings on the topic have taken the form of government reports related to the activities of specific national metrology laboratories. This book is the first systematic study of measurement activity at a national metrology laboratory, and the laboratory studied is the U.S. National Institute of Standards and Technology (NIST) within the U.S. Department of Commerce.

The primary objective of the book is to emphasize for academic and policy audiences the economic importance of measurement not only as an area of study but also as a tool for sustaining technological advancement as an element of economic growth. Toward this goal, the book offers an overview of the economic benefits and consequences of measurement standards; an argument for public sector support of measurement standards; a historical perspective of the measurement activities at NIST; an empirical analysis of one particular measurement activity at NIST, namely calibration testing; and a roadmap for future research on the economics of metrology.

Albert N. Link is the Virginia Batte Phillips Distinguished Professor at the University of North Carolina at Greensboro, United States.

Routledge Studies in Economic Theory, Method and Philosophy

False Feedback in Economics
The Case for Replication
Andrin Spescha

The Economics and Science of Measurement
A Study of Metrology
Albert N. Link

For more information about this series, please visit: www.routledge.com/Routledge-Studies-in-Economic-Theory-Method-and-Philosophy/book-series/RSEMTP

The Economics and Science of Measurement

A Study of Metrology

Albert N. Link

LONDON AND NEW YORK

First published 2022
by Routledge
2 Park Square, Milton Park, Abingdon, Oxon OX14 4RN

and by Routledge
605 Third Avenue, New York, NY 10158

Routledge is an imprint of the Taylor & Francis Group, an informa business

British Library Cataloguing-in-Publication Data
A catalogue record for this book is available from the British Library

Library of Congress Cataloging-in-Publication Data
Names: Link, Albert N., author.
Title: The economics and science of measurement: a study of metrology/
Albert N. Link.
Description: Milton Park, Abingdon, Oxon; New York, NY: Routledge,
2022. |
Series: Routledge studies in economic theory, method and philosophy |
Includes bibliographical references and index.
Subjects: LCSH: Metrology–Economic aspects. | Measurement.
Classification: LCC QC91 .L49 2022 (print) | LCC QC91 (ebook) |
DDC 389/.15–dc23
LC record available at https://lccn.loc.gov/2021014888
LC ebook record available at https://lccn.loc.gov/2021014889

ISBN: 978-1-032-01440-1 (hbk)
ISBN: 978-1-032-03367-9 (pbk)
ISBN: 978-1-003-18695-3 (ebk)

Typeset in Times New Roman
by Deanta Global Publishing Services, Chennai, India

Contents

Figures

Tables

Acknowledgements

I am indebted to my colleague Martijn van Hasselt for his many helpful comments and suggestions on papers that formed the framework for this book. I am also indebted to my virtual colleagues, Cristiano Antonelli (University of Turin), John Scott (Dartmouth College), and Greg Tassey (University of Washington and former Chief Economist at the National Institute of Standards and Technology), for sharing their insight and encouragement about earlier versions of this book.

I am also grateful to the scholarship of the many accomplished authors who are cited herein from whom I have learned much and will continue to do so.

I also appreciate the University of North Carolina at Greensboro for awarding me a research assignment (i.e., a sabbatical) during the fall semester of 2020 to pursue this project.

About the author

Albert N. Link is the Virginia Batte Phillips Distinguished Professor at the University of North Carolina at Greensboro (UNCG). He received the B.S. degree in mathematics from the University of Richmond (Phi Beta Kappa) and the Ph.D. degree in economics from Tulane University. After receiving the Ph.D., he joined the economics faculty at Auburn University, was later Scholar-in-Residence at Syracuse University, and then he joined the economics faculty at UNCG in 1982. In 2019, Link was awarded the title and honorary position of Visiting Professor at Northumbria University, U.K.

Professor Link's research focuses on technology and innovation policy, the economics of R&D, and policy / program evaluation. He is currently the Editor-in-Chief of the *Journal of Technology Transfer*. He is also co-editor of *Foundations and Trends in Entrepreneurship* and founder / editor of *Annals of Science and Technology Policy*.

Among his more than 65 books, some of the more recent ones are: *Collaborative Research in the United States: Policies and Institutions for Cooperation among Firms* (Routledge, 2020), *Invention, Innovation and U.S. Federal Laboratories* (Edward Elgar, 2020), *Technology Transfer and U.S. Public Sector Innovation* (Edward Elgar, 2020), *Sources of Knowledge and Entrepreneurial Behavior* (University of Toronto Press, 2019), *Handbook for University Technology Transfer* (University of Chicago Press, 2015), *Public Sector Entrepreneurship: U.S. Technology and Innovation Policy* (Oxford University Press, 2015), *Bending the Arc of Innovation: Public Support of R&D in Small, Entrepreneurial Firms* (Palgrave Macmillan 2013), *Valuing an Entrepreneurial Enterprise* (Oxford University Press, 2012), *Public Goods, Public Gains: Calculating the Social Benefits of Public R&D* (Oxford University Press, 2011), *Employment Growth from Public Support of Innovation in Small Firms* (W.E. Upjohn Institute for Employment Research, 2011), and *Government as Entrepreneur* (Oxford University Press, 2009).

Professor Link's other research endeavours consist of more than 200 peer-reviewed journal articles and book chapters, as well as numerous government reports. His scholarship has appeared in such journals as the *American Economic Review*, the *Journal of Political Economy*, the *Review of Economics and Statistics*, *Economica*, *Research Policy*, *Economics of Innovation and New Technology*, the *European Economic Review*, *Small Business Economics*, *ISSUES in Science and Technology*, *Scientometrics*, and the *Journal of Technology Transfer*.

Professor Link's public service includes being a member of the National Research Council's research team that conducted the 2010 evaluation of the U.S. Small Business Innovation Research (SBIR) program. Based on that assignment, he testified before the U.S. Congress in April 2011 on the economic benefits associated with the SBIR program. Link also served from 2007 to 2012 as a U.S. Representative to the United Nations (in Geneva) in the capacity of co-vice chairperson of the Team of Specialists on Innovation and Competitiveness Policies Initiative for the Economic Commission for Europe. In October 2018, Link delivered the European Commission Distinguished Scholar Lecture at the European Commission's Joint Research Centre (in Seville).

1 Introduction

Why the economics of metrology?

Metrology, the study of measurement science, is certainly not a mainstream topic within economics, or for that matter within either the social science or public policy disciplines. To wit: few if any journals within these disciplines include metrology as a field of interest in their statement of aims and goals, and there are no *Journal of Economics Literature* (JEL) classifications specific to the economics of metrology.[1] It is thus not an unreasonable question for the reader to ask: why read about the economics of metrology? Or stated differently: why would an economist, a social scientist, or a public policy scholar want to learn about metrology? With the above statements as background, these are not unreasonable questions, but there are at least four appropriate answers to these questions.[2]

First, to dispel any preconceptions, the economics of metrology is in fact an area that has not been totally ignored by economists, social scientists, or public policy scholars; it is, from my vantage point, simply an understudied area.[3] However, much of what has been written about the economics of metrology or the economics of measurement science does not often reveal itself in traditional journals in these fields of study. However, discussions and analyses of measurement standards do occupy important places in numerous government reports from many different countries, and the topic of metrology has not been infrequently addressed by scholars in archaeological and institutional history journals. Regarding the relevant government reports, the authors of such reports have generally been trained in areas within the above fields of study; regarding the history journals, the authors of that body of scholarship perhaps unwittingly have provided very important context for the former.

There are two dimensions of the economics of the science of measurement to consider. There is the technical content of measurement science which is based on the underlying research associated with, for example, standards,

DOI: 10.4324/9781003186953-1

and there is the applied content of measurement science that is revealed through the implementation or use of standards (Tassey, 2017). There are premier journals, such as the *Journal of Scientific and Industrial Metrology*, *Measurement*, *Metrologia*, and others, that emphasize the technical content of measurement science. It is, as I view the literature, the economics of the applied content of measurement science that is relatively under-researched from an economics as well as from a policy perspective.

Second, countries invest billions of public sector dollars in measurement science. Public sector dollars originate with taxpayers, and those dollars like all public resources have alternative uses for the intended betterment of society. But still, the public sector in many countries has remained committed to the social importance of measurement science. While data on country-by-country investments in measurement science are not always readily available, there are selected data on dimensions of those investments that have been made in the United States, and the magnitude of those investments is substantial. Taxpayers thus deserve to know about the economic consequences of such expenditures, and a public accountability criterion necessitates that the public sector document information about the economic consequences of such expenditures.

The national metrology laboratory in the United States is the National Institute of Standards and Technology (NIST). NIST is administratively located within the U.S. Department of Commerce.[4] NIST's operating budget in fiscal year FY 2020 was just over $1 billion, and that fact alone might be a sufficient reason for one to learn more about the economics of the measurement science that occurs within NIST.[5] Using the level of such an investment as a justification for learning more about metrology, one might recall, with tongue in cheek of course, the following statement that has been attributed to the former U.S. Congressman and Senator from the State of Illinois, Everett Dirksen: "A billion here, a billion there, and pretty soon you're talking real money."[6]

Third, measurement is everywhere; it is pervasive throughout many disciplines, and economics is no exception.[7] Many economists, and perhaps it would be fair even to say most economists, would simply not succeed empirically in their discipline without precise and accurate measurement of critical economic variables. For example, economists in general rely on the accuracy of measures of Gross Domestic Product (GDP), employment and unemployment statistics and their percentage changes, inflation rates, citation counts, journal impact factors, and the list goes on and on. To be more precise, scholars in health economics base many of their empirical studies on precisely and accurately measured drug dosage treatment inputs as well as measured outcomes through standardized vital statistics, those in environmental economics base many of their empirical studies on precisely and accurately measured emission levels, and those in innovation economics base many of their empirical studies on precisely and accurately measured patent counts and levels of investment in research and development (R&D).[8]

And fourth, from a historical perspective, the words of John Quincy Adams, the sixth president of the United States, are as relevant today as they were in 1821:[9]

> Weights and measures may be ranked among the necessaries of life to every individual of human society. They enter into the economical arrangements and daily concerns of every family. They are necessary to every occupation of human industry; to the distribution and security of every species of property; to every transaction of trade and commerce; to the labors of the husbandman; to the ingenuity of the artificer; to the studies of the philosopher; to the researches of the antiquarian, to the navigation of the mariner, and the marches of the soldier; to all the exchanges of peace, and all the operations of war. The knowledge of them, as in established use, is among the first elements of education, and is often learned by those who learn nothing else, not even to read and write. This knowledge is riveted in the memory by the habitual application of it to the employments of men throughout life.

What exactly will an economist, social scientist, or public policy scholar relate to from a study of metrology? As an answer to this question, one interpretation of the economics of the subject matter is offered below.[10]

The origin of measurement

The measurement of actions and events predates modern economic theory. Himbert (2009) suggested that the first economic use of measurement might trace as far back in time as to the activities that are claimed to have occurred in Mesopotamia in 6000 BC. Himbert (2009, p. 26) wrote:

> Among the oldest testimonies of measurement processes in the mid-eastern civilisations, one has to mention the clay balls (6000 BC) found in Mesopotamia: to assess for instance the size of a flock of sheep, the owner was sealing into a large clay sphere as many small balls as there were individuals in the flock (e.g. lambs). The seal was broken, if necessary, to give reliable evidence of the earlier characteristics of the flock.

Measurement in 6000 BC relied totally on counting: 1, 2, 3, and so forth. Himbert aptly places this anecdotal information about clay balls in juxtaposition to the wisdom of Lord (William Thomson) Kelvin, perhaps as a limpid reminder to readers that the purpose of measurement is to give reliable knowledge on objects or concepts.[11] In Lord Kelvin's May 3, 1883, lecture to the Institution of Civil Engineers, it has been acknowledged that he said:[12]

> I often say that when you can measure what you are speaking about, and express it in numbers, you know something about it; but when you cannot measure it, when you cannot express it in numbers, your knowledge is of a meagre and unsatisfactory kind; it may be the beginning of knowledge, but you have scarcely in your thoughts advanced to the state of Science, whatever the matter may be.

However, the measurement of economic variables is not the same as the economics of measurement, meaning the economic implications of being able to measure something with precision and accuracy.[13,14]

This book is about the economics of the science of measurement.[15] The economics of measurement is in fact a topic area about which much has been written, although little of which is likely known to the average student of either the science or art of economics.

Swann (2009) has appropriately placed the economics of measurement in an epistemological context by pointing out that the topic had been addressed by several of the classical economists who not only made reference to measurement *per se* but also from whom there were inferences about the economic importance of the science of measurement.[16]

To draw directly from Swann's (2009) seminal report, Adam Smith, in *An Inquiry into the Nature and Causes of the Wealth of Nations* (1776/1914, p. 18), commenting on the economic benefits of maritime trade, made reference for the need of measurement for that trade to be efficient and thus effective for economic growth:

> The nations that, according to the best authenticated history, appear to have been first civilised, were those that dwelt round the coast of the Mediterranean Sea. That sea, by far the greatest inlet that is known in the world, having no tides, nor consequently any waves except such as are caused by the wind only was, by the smoothness of its surface, as well as by the multitude of its islands, and the proximity of its neighbouring shores, extremely favourable to the infant navigation of the world; when, from their *ignorance of the compass* [emphasis added], men were afraid to quit the view of the coast, and from the imperfection of the art of shipbuilding, to abandon themselves to the boisterous waves of the ocean.

Swann (2009, p. 12), commented on this particular passage from Smith in the following way:

> By implication, trade by the more ambitious trading routes only became possible with the advent of the compass. The example gives the compass a prominent place as a measurement instrument which reduces the risk of navigation.

As well, Alfred Marshall, in *Industry and Trade* (1920, p. 201), pointed out the importance of standardized measurement in the context of industrial production, and he hinted not only about the production benefits of standardized measurement but also about its public good nature:

> General standardization for industrial purposes is sometimes set up at a stroke by authority of Government, or of a convention of leaders in the industries most directly concerned. Thus, for instance, the present electrical standards, Watt, Ohm, Ampère, etc. were fixed by an international convention: and every Government appoints, and charges from time to time, the exact measurements and other specifications of rifle cartridges, whether made in its own or in private workshops. No one would assert that the general adoption of standards, differing by a little from any of these, would be much less useful: but there is a vast advantage in the existence of definite standards, adhesion to which within less than a thousandth part may be required in certain cases.

As a summary statement, which will be elaborated on throughout this book, measurement science has an economic role which is, at its most general level, to support a set of technologies that perform an infrastructure role in the economy. This infrastructure role has public good characteristics, which thus implies a rationale for a related public sector or government or policy intervention.

Overview of the book

In Chapter 2 of this book, the economic benefits and consequences of measurement science, as reflected through measurement standards, are discussed. In that chapter, references are made to contemporary mainstream theories and topic areas in economics to which measurement standards apply. Chapter 2 concludes with a mathematical model of the decision process of a firm that contemplates using measurement standards in its production activities.

The role of the public sector to provide measurement standards—a public good—is the topic of Chapter 3. The role of the public sector in the conduct of measurement science and in the subsequent provision of measurement standards is based on the economics principle of market failure. In the United States, the supply of measurement standards is fulfilled by the activities that take place at NIST, but most other countries have national metrology laboratories that also supply measurement standards. A brief history of NIST is presented in this chapter, and the mission of the metrology laboratories in other countries is identified for reference, but not for discussion purposes.

Several different measurement standards related outputs that result from the publicly funded measurement science research within the research laboratory divisions at NIST are defined and summarized in Chapter 4. These outputs include the NIST staff who participated with standards organizations in the process of developing documentary standards, standard reference data, standard reference materials, and calibration tests.

Calibration tests—and calibrations embody measurement standards—performed at NIST are considered in more detail in Chapter 5. Calibration tests are the focus of this chapter for a pragmatic reason, namely detailed data were provided by NIST on a number of dimensions of their calibration testing program, and those data lend themselves to an exploratory presentation of stylized facts about calibration testing at the U.S. metrology laboratory.

This book concludes in Chapter 6 with summary remarks and a roadmap for possible future research on the topic of the economics and science of measurement—a study of metrology.[17]

Notes

1 There are publications in the field of econometrics that address measurement issues, but these data-based discussions do not address economic considerations such as a definition of a scientific measurement method, the supply of scientific measurement methods, the demand for scientific measurement methods, or even the market for scientific measurement methods.

2 This book is an elaboration on earlier ideas that are in Link (2021). There is some overlap of the contextual information in Link (2021) and the material herein.

3 To paraphrase from an anonymous reviewer's critique of what became Link (2021), the economics of metrology can be considered the less famous, and younger, sibling of the economics of standardization. After the pioneering work by Hemenway and David, and others, in the 1970s and early 1980s, as reviewed by David and Greenstein (1990), the economics of standardization took off as an important area of economic theory, and later as an important area of applied microeconomics. However, the research field of the economics of metrology is not nearly as well developed.

4 See www.nist.gov/ (accessed on January 2, 2021).
5 See www.nist.gov/fy2021-presidential-budget-request-summary (accessed on January 2, 2021).
6 See www.everettdirksen.name/print_emd_billionhere.htm (accessed on January 3, 2021).
7 Michell (2005) discussed the importance of measurement from a scientific method perspective.
8 Economists also conceptually measure (i.e., count) variables such as an individual's utils of satisfaction from consumption.
9 This passage is quoted from Richardson (1976, p. 1).
10 Plato wrote in *The Republic* the following, "The beginning is the most important part of the work."
11 See https://digital.nls.uk/scientists/biographies/lord-kelvin/ (accessed November 1, 2020).
12 See www.gilb.com/blog/when-you-can-measure-what-you-are-speaking-about-and-express-it-in-numbers-you-know-something-about-it (accessed November 2, 2020).
13 See Richardson (1976) for an excellent history of measurement systems. See also Porter (2001).
14 Harris and Harris (1996, p. 75) wrote: "measures themselves came about in response to emerging needs to measure with varying degrees of accuracy the commodities that were traded in society."
15 As noted above, the motivation for this book comes from an earlier exploratory study on the impact of measurement science on U.S. productivity. Some contextual material from that study is repeated herein. See Link (2021).
16 This section borrows directly from Swann's (2009) insight about these classical scholars. This material is emphasized in Link (2021).
17 William Blake wrote in *The Marriage of Heaven and Hell*: "You never know what is enough unless you know what is more than enough."

2 The economic benefits and consequences of measurement standards

The two sections in this chapter that follow are related to the economic benefits of measurement standards and to the attendant economic consequences of measurement standards. At the end of this chapter, the two concepts of benefits and consequences are related to each other through an equilibrium model that characterizes the calculus of a firm's adoption (from the demand side) of measurement standards.

Economic benefits

Measurement standards, which lead to standardization, benefit both intermediate and final consumers as well as related producers throughout the relevant supply chains.[1] As with any economic activity, incentives are at play. Not only will consumers and producers participate in the measurement standards' setting processes to the extent to which they will benefit from doing so, but also consumers and producers will participate in the adoption of standards to the extent to which they too will benefit (Link, 1983). The mathematical model at the end of this chapter, which is based on the assumption that the supply of measurement standards is given, represents an effort to formalize an equilibrium situation where the marginal benefits to a firm from adopting a measurement standard are equal to the marginal cost of doing so.[2] The equilibrium solution to this model is referenced again in Chapter 5 to define or interpret the relevance of the NIST related data that are explored descriptively therein.

Transactions between, as well as among, consumers and producers are never perfect. There are always information asymmetries to some degree, and measurement standards benefit both parties by reducing such information asymmetries; however, information asymmetries are not always completely removed.[3]

From the perspective of consumers, reduced uncertainty about the characteristics and usefulness of a product might reduce the effective price of

DOI: 10.4324/9781003186953-2

the product because search costs will have decreased. If consumer confidence about a product increases because of the reduced uncertainty, the market price of the product might also fall due to an increase in the overall demand as well as supply of the product.

From the perspective of producers, production costs might fall as variety deduction is reduced with measurement standards. As a result, scale economies might likely increase, consumer confidence might also again increase, and thus the size of the market will possibly increase as well.

Tassey (2017) wrote about the economic benefits of measurement standards in a related way. He defined four benefit categories from measurement standards. These categories are production efficiency, product structure, system integration, and commercialization. Specifically, Tassey wrote (2017, p. 225):

> Efficiency in production requires standardized process models and performance metrics to control fabrication processes for quality and yield.[4]
>
> Where large economies of scale are important, product variety reduction may be necessary to lower unit costs, thereby achieving acceptable price points.
>
> Producing effectively functioning systems of hardware and software components requires standard specifications of system performance and standardized interfaces to allow sufficient competition and maximum innovation at the component level and access to critical information networks.
>
> Because buyers require assurances of adequate component and system performance before consummating purchases, innovation and especially subsequent market penetration require cost-effective, product-acceptance standards.

Robertson's and Swanepoel's (2015) views about the economic benefits from standardized measurement align well with the Tassey viewpoints mentioned above. These two authors emphasized the economic benefits of limiting market failure, reducing transaction costs, increasing economic efficiency, and supporting innovation. To represent precisely their manner of description, consider the following passage from their 2015 report to the Australian Government entitled *The Economics of Metrology* (pp. 8–9):

> Asymmetric information between buyers and sellers is one of the most common sources of market failure, which occurs when the buyer cannot determine the quality of a product and as a result does not purchase the product.

> Transaction costs arise as a result of the information between consumers and producers being asymmetric and incomplete. By having an agreed standard of measurement, a buyer can spend less time searching for goods and incur fewer costs associated with checking that the product conforms to the quality requirements. In addition to this, producers can also reduce their transaction costs [normally incurred at the transaction stage, i.e., buying and selling] by producing a product that complies with the standard. By producing a product in accordance with the standard, a producer can incur fewer costs associated with correcting defects to meet specifications, which allows for the product to be certified and also leads to trust regarding the certification and performance of the product compared to a competitor's product.
>
> Measurement increases economic efficiency by creating economies of scale. In the context of economies of scale, measurement standards have the ability to reduce variety in that standards can set limits to a fixed number of product characteristics. By limiting the number of characteristics a product has, this lowers the costs associated with the production of one unit of the good for suppliers, since they do not need to produce a heterogeneous good for different consumers.
>
> Measurement plays a role in supporting and stimulating innovation, collaboration, and commercialisation. Measurement is considered to be one of the infra-technologies, thus one of the technologies that provide the technical infrastructure and tools necessary for further innovation. Measurement and standards do this by providing [or at least facilitating] a platform on which new technologies and processes can be built on and demonstrated.

Finally, Swann's views about the economic benefits of measurement standards are also in agreement with the views summarized above, and his perspective emphasized benefits to both consumers and producers. To represent precisely his viewpoint, consider the following passage from his 2009 report to the then National Measurement and Regulation Office in London (dissolved in 2016) entitled *The Economics of Metrology and Measurement* (pp. iv–v) in which he emphasizes distinctive elements of measurement science:

> The use of measurement can increase the productivity of organisations ... The more precise is the measurement and the more rapid is the feedback from measurement to control, the greater are the effects on efficiency, quality and productivity.[5]
>
> Measurement supports innovation ... Measurement is also important to the innovator as it offers an objective way to demonstrate to customers that an innovative product is indeed superior to the competition.[6]

> Improvements in measurement can help to reduce the transaction costs between suppliers and customers in a market economy. One of the most common sources of market failure is asymmetric information between buyers and sellers, where the buyer cannot distinguish good products from bad and therefore does not buy. Often this arises because measurement is difficult or expensive. As measurement improves and becomes cheaper, then buyers can measure any product characteristics they wish to, and that eliminates the asymmetric information and reduces the transaction costs.
>
> Measurement can help a broader group of beneficiaries … Many consumers are interested in careful measurement of product characteristics to ensure quality, safety, purity, dosage accuracy and so on … In the health service, clinicians depend on the precise measurement of doses, which is essential for efficacy and safety in medicines and for the diagnosis of medical conditions. They also make extensive use of measurement instruments to check patient health (blood pressure, blood tests, and so on) … Those concerned with the environment depend on measurement for accurate information about meteorological conditions (wind, rainfall, sunshine, temperature, etc.), pollution and emissions (including carbon dioxide emissions), geo-seismic measures, measures of the ozone layer, measures of the condition of the polar caps, and so on … Measurement has at least three important roles in education and training: as part of the curriculum, as an essential input to the research process, and in assessing student aptitude and performance.

With regard to the four views summarized above (my own view, Tassey's view, Robertson and Swanepoel's view, and the view by Swann),[7] there are at least three overarching themes about the economic benefits of standardized measurement that emerge, and these three themes are related to one another. The first theme is that standardized measurement alleviates *information asymmetry* [emphasis added] between consumers and producers. The second theme is that standardized measurement reduces *transaction costs* [emphasis added] among consumers and producers (with a reminder that an intermediate goods consumer in period 1 can be a producer in a supply chain in period 2). And, the third theme is that standardized measurement brings about *efficiency* [emphasis added], namely process efficiency. These three themes are not necessarily independent of each other.

A hallmark publication in the economics literature on information asymmetry is Akerlof's 1970 article entitled "The Market for 'Lemons': Quality Uncertainty and the Market Mechanism."[8] Therein, Akerlof argues, as well as demonstrates mathematically, that bad will drive out good. To illustrate this conclusion, Akerlof references automobile dealers. An automobile dealer relies on specific information, and thus the dealer knows better than a consumer where to hide flaws in an automobile. A consumer relies on general information, and thus the consumer will not likely be able to identify all of the flaws known to a dealer. Through measurement standards, the consumer will at least know that the components of the automobile are within manufacturing guidelines (otherwise the manufacturer of the automobile would not have reached a purchasing agreement with the supplier of the particular components) and thus some degree of uncertainty, that is, of information asymmetry, will have been reduced.

Regarding transaction costs, Williamson's 1979 article, "Transaction Cost Economics: The Governance of Contractual Relations," arguably might have been the single publication that popularized the concept (in the field of economics in particular) that internal costs versus transaction costs are related to the governance structure of a firm and thus to the growth potential of the firm.[9] More broadly speaking in terms of measurement standards, there are costs (e.g., time, background research, independent measurements) associated with two parties engaging in a transaction. From the perspective of a producer who purchases a critical component from a supplier, if the component's measurable dimensions are traceable to a standard that is widely accepted—a national standard—then independent verification of the measured dimensions is not needed, or if needed, verification on a very limited basis would be required. The economic savings to each party of the transaction for not having to make an independent verification means that transaction costs will have decreased, and as a result the transaction will likely be consummated. The reduction in transaction costs results from a reduction in information uncertainty.

Economic consequences

There have been a number of excellent reviews of the published literature related to the economic and institutional consequences of measurement standards (e.g., Birch, 2003; DTI, 2005; Swann, 2009, 2010; Lambert, 2010; Stokes et al., 2011; Robertson and Swanepoel, 2015; Spencer and Temple, 2016; King et al., 2017; Blind et al., 2020, 2011; Foucart and Li, 2021).[10] These reports and published empirical studies are not only important from a descriptive perspective for general consumption but also from a leveraging perspective to help to justify future public sector investments in measurement standards. These reports and empirical studies that the referenced authors summarize are often based on, at least in part, an empirical model of the general form:

$$Performance = \mathrm{f}\left(Stock\ of\ Standards, \mathbf{X}\right) \tag{2.1}$$

where the variable *Performance* has been measured in terms of an accepted (i.e., standardized) aggregate economic performance variable at period *t* such as total factor productivity, the variable *Stock of Standards* is a count variable of the number of existing national measurement standards at period *t*, and **X** is a vector of time-related controls such as national expenditure toward R&D. Within this body of research, the estimated coefficient on the variable *Stock of Standards* from varying specifications of the function form of f(·) is positive and statistically significant at varying levels of significance thus suggesting an aggregate relationship between economic performance and investments in measurement standards as reflected through the stock of measurement standards.[11]

There is yet another body of literature to consider, one that for the most part has been centred around the activities in the United States. These studies identify a particular public sector funded measurement standard, and then the authors calculate (the calculations are frequently based on interview information) the social benefits that can be identified as being associated with the public sector's investment in the measurement standard being studied. Many of these studies have been published as chapters in authored or edited volumes, although a few have been published in academic journals (e.g., Link, 1996; Link and Scott, 1998, 2011, 2012, 2019).[12]

NIST, the national metrology laboratory in the United States that funded a number of such evaluation studies, has summarized a portion of these studies that it commissioned in an effort to document the economic consequences of measurement standards. The measurement standards considered included, but were not limited to, performance standards, test methods, and standard reference data. Table 2.1 briefly summarizes the findings from the NIST studies that were completed over the 1981 through 2009 time period.[13] One might reach a similar conclusion from these studies as from the studies based on the estimation of variants of equation (2.1); measurement standards do matter from the perspective of enhancing economic growth and the commonweal.

To illustrate the scope of these NIST funded evaluation studies that are listed in Table 2.1, consider as a representative example the laser and fibreoptic power and energy calibration services study (TASC, 2000 pp. ES1–ES3):[14]

> Laser output power/energy is used to specify the characteristics of lasers and laser systems, and industry has recognized the importance of accurate calibrations of instruments measuring that output with traceability to national (primary) standards established and maintained at NIST … [T]he use of power meters calibrated to absolute standards at NIST is intrinsic to [for example] economical semiconductor

Table 2.1 NIST-sponsored studies of the consequences of alternative measurement standards (1981–2009)

Industry / technology	*Year*	*Measurement standard*	*Economic outcome*
Semiconductors: resistivity	1981	Test methods	Increase productivity
Semiconductors: thermal conductivity	1981	Materials properties test methods	Increase R&D efficiency, lower transaction costs
Semiconductors: wire bonding	1981	Test methods	Increase productivity, increase R&D efficiency
Communications: electromagnetic interference	1991	Test methods	Lower transaction costs
Semiconductors: electromigration	1992	Test methods	Increase R&D efficiency, lower transactions costs
Photonics: optical fibre	1992	Test methods (acceptance)	Lower transaction costs
Automation: real-time control systems	1995	Generic architecture	Increase R&D efficiency
Energy: electric meter calibration	1995	Test methods (calibration)	Lower transaction costs
Communications: ISDN	1995	Interoperability standards	Lower transaction costs
Computers: software conformance	1995	Test methods (acceptance)	Lower transaction costs
Photonics: spectral irradiance	1995	Test method (calibration)	Increase productivity, lower transaction costs
Construction: building codes	1996	Technical basis for standards	Energy conservation, energy cost savings
Construction: roofing shingles	1996	Materials properties	Increase durability
Construction: fire safety evaluation systems	1996	Technical basis for standards	Lower compliance costs
Automation: machine tool software error compensation	1996	Quality control algorithm	Increase R&D efficiency, increase productivity
Materials: thermocouples	1997	Standard reference data (calibration)	Lower transaction costs increase product quality
Pharmaceuticals: radiopharmaceuticals	1997	Standard reference materials	Increase product quality
Photonics: optical detector calibration	1997	Standards and calibration services	Increase productivity
Chemicals: alternative refrigerants	1998	Standard reference data	Increase R&D efficiency, increase productivity
Materials: phase equilibria for advanced ceramics	1998	Standard reference data	Increase R&D efficiency, increase productivity

Semiconductors: software for design automation (IGBT semiconductors)	1999	Software model	Increase R&D efficiency, increase productivity
Pharmaceuticals: cholesterol measurement	2000	Standard reference materials	Increase productivity, decrease transaction costs
Photonics: laser and fibreoptic power and energy calibration	2000	Calibrations	Increase productivity, decrease transaction costs
Electronics: Josephson voltage standard	2001	Standard reference materials	Increase R&D efficiency. increase productivity, enable new markets
Chemicals: SRMs for sulphur in fossil fuels	2000	Standard reference materials	Increase productivity, reduce transaction costs
Communications: security (data encryption standards)	2001	Standard conformance test methods/ services	Increase R&D efficiency, enable new markets
Communications: security (role-based access control)	2001	Generic technology reference models	Enable new markets, increase R&D efficiency
Chemicals: National Traceable Reference Materials Program (NTRM)	2002	Reference data; calibration services	Increase efficiency of regulatory compliance (content and production efficiencies for standards)
Manufacturing: standards for product data exchange (STEP)	2002	Standards development; conformance test methods/services	Increase quality and assimilation of standards, accelerate standards development
Semiconductors: models and techniques for superfilling	2008	Models and techniques for research	Increase R&D efficiency
Semiconductors: characterization data for low-k materials	2008	Materials characterization	Increase R&D, production, and technology adoption efficiency
Materials: combinatorial methods consortium	2009	Combinatorial methods for polymer research	Increase R&D efficiency and technology transfer

Source: www.nist.gov/director/outputs-and-outcomes-nist-laboratory-research (accessed November 29, 2020).

> production. Such traceability to standards ensures integrity and reliability of laser measurement, and the reduced measurement uncertainty lessens the dependence on the experimental method of semiconductor process development and production. Also, a power meter traceable to NIST's primary standards reduces the time spent troubleshooting photolithography problems because engineers have greater confidence in the accuracy of the detector readings.

As well, consider as another representative example the study of standard reference materials for sulphur in fossil fuels (RTI, 2000, pp. ES2–ES4):

> Technical issues elevate the importance of accuracy and precision in the measurement of sulfur content. The primary environmental concern is sulfur dioxide (SO_2), which is produced from the combustion of fuels that contain sulfur as an impurity ... Without the development of the isotope dilution thermal ionization mass spectrometry (IDMS) method [at NIST], sulfur measurement in industry would be subject to greater bias and uncertainty.

A model of firm adoption of measurement standards

Consider the following mathematical model related to the use of a measurement standard by a manufacturing firm. In essence, when a firm adopts a measurement standard, the firm is in effect capturing new infrastructural knowledge. For the adopting firm, this new knowledge is embodied in the measurement standard that has perceived value to the firm but that the firm cannot develop (i.e., at a reasonable cost) on its own. The measurement standard is provided at a cost (lower than the cost for the firm to develop it on its own) by a third party, and the third party could reasonably be referred to as a public sector metrology laboratory, or simply as the public sector.[15] It should not be overlooked that the measurement standard itself is promulgated by the private sector (e.g., firms in industry).[16]

In this model, a two-step decision process is assumed to be used by the firm. First, the firm decides whether or not to adopt a measurement standard; and second, having decided to adopt a measurement standard, the firm decides how pervasive its use of the measurement standard will be.[17]

The value to the firm from adopting a measurement standard is twofold. The measurement standard increases the probability that, among other things, the manufacturing process within the firm will be more successful than without the measurement standard, and the measurement standard will increase the market value of any manufacturing output that might result because of reduced information asymmetries and transaction costs.

Let the probability (p) that the manufacturing process results in a successfully marketable output (Q) be represented by the concave function $p(q)$, where q indicates the quality or marketability of the output.[18] Also, let the net revenues, R, associated with the production and sale of the resulting output be represented by the concave function $R(q)$.

Let the scope of use of the measurement standard be represented by S, where S might be thought of empirically as a newly defined input in the production process. The quality, q, of the output, Q, is itself assumed to be a concave function, $q(S)$, of the level of use of the measurement standard. Thus, the expected (e) net revenues from the production and sale of the resulting output will be a function of S:[19]

$$R^e = p(q(S)) \cdot R(q(S)), \tag{2.2}$$

and the marginal net expected revenues (MR_S) per unit of the metric for the scope of the firm's activities that use the measurement standard in the production and sale of the output will be:[20]

$$MR_S = p(q(S)) \cdot R'(q(S)) + R(q(S)) \cdot p'(q(S)). \tag{2.3}$$

There are, of course, costs to using a measurement standard both in terms of the physical and intellectual effort required to integrate the measurement standard into the manufacturing process as well as the *per se* costs of the measurement standard. Assuming that these costs include both fixed and variable components, the cost function (c) can be represented as:[21]

$$c = c(S) \text{ where } c(0) > 0,\ c'(S) > 0, \text{ and } c''(S) > 0. \tag{2.4}$$

The optimal level of use of a measurement standard,[22] assuming the firm seeks to maximize the expected level of profit (π) from integrating a measurement standard, will be some S^* that maximizes the expected profits associated with the process of integrating the standard:

$$\pi^e(S) = p(q(S)) \cdot R(q(S)) - c(S), \tag{2.5}$$

that is, S^* will be that level of S that equates marginal net expected revenue, MR_S, to the marginal cost, MC, of the measurement standard integrating process:

$$p(q(S)) \cdot R'(q(S)) + R(q(S)) \cdot p'(q(S)) = c'(S). \tag{2.6}$$

This final relationship is not used explicitly in the remainder of this book to describe the firms and organizations from which data are available on calibration testing. Rather, the point of the model is that the firm would integrate measurement metrology to the extent that the marginal benefit from doing so equals the marginal cost of doing so.[23]

In Chapter 3, an argument for the public sector to support the provision of measurement standards is discussed with reference to the concept of market failure.

Notes

1 The arguments that follow, some of which are paraphrased, were greatly influenced by Swann (2009, 2010), Robertson and Swanepoel (2015), Allen (1999), Barzel (1982), and the other authors discussed and cited below.

2 This model, which follows directly from Link (2021), assumes that the use of standardized measurement (legal measurement or metrology) is a voluntary choice. "Legal metrology is that part of metrology which is subject to legal/regulatory control. It is defined in the *International Vocabulary of Legal Metrology* as that part of metrology relating to activities which result from statutory requirements and concern measurement, units of measurement, measuring instruments and methods of measurement and which are performed by competent bodies" (International Trade Centre, 2004, p. 1). See also Filho and Gonçalves (2015) for a discussion of legal metrology. Legal metrology is referenced again several times in Chapter 3, Table 3.1.

3 As Barzel (1982, p. 28) noted: "Virtually no commodity offered for sale is free from the cost of measuring its attributes." See also Klaes (2000).

4 The Department of Business, Energy & Industrial Strategy's (2017) report emphasizes the productivity benefits from measurement as well.

5 See Savio et al. (2016) for examples related to Danish manufacturing. Jula (2001) discusses this point with reference to the semiconductor industry.

6 Kaarls (2007, p. 435) wrote: "Sustainable competitiveness and innovation require accurate, traceable measurement results."

7 These are complementary views, and they are presented in juxtaposition with no intention of creating an invidious comparison.

8 The following sections about Akerlof and Williamson draw on the insight of Swann (2009).

9 See also Allen (1999).

10 With few exceptions, the studies referenced in these reviews are government or institute reports and not articles in academic journals. There are of course exceptions to this generalization; see for example Temple and Williams (2002) and Choudhary et al. (2013).

11 There is a dearth of such aggregate studies that are relevant to the aggregate performance of the United States. One exception is Link (2021).

12 Rather than asking how a particular measurement standard benefits an interviewed respondent's firm, one could ask the interview respondent questions that allow understanding how the firm's R&D investments would differ if metrology standards (whichever ones are relevant for the respondent) were unavailable.

That approach is developed and used in the metrology standards portion of Scott and Scott (2015).

13 The National Bureau of Economic Research (NBER) has dated the Great Recession to have occurred in the United States from December 2007 through June 2009. Perhaps the financial impact of the Great Recession caused a slowdown in the provision of additional studies of the type summarized in Table 2.1.

14 This study can be accessed at www.nist.gov/tpo/nist-economic-impact-studies-table.

15 The public sector does not develop standards in isolation from the private sector's needs. Many standards are consensus standards. So, my use of the term *third party* should be interpreted to refer to an amalgam of organizations.

16 Data are presented in Chapter 4 that illustrate the number of NIST staff that work with organizations to promulgate industrial standards.

17 This model draws, in part, from Audretsch, Leyden, and Link (2012). This model, as it relates to calibration tests, is presented and discussed in Link (2021).

18 The term *concave* refers to the first derivative of the function being positive, and the second derivative being negative.

19 The firm will choose the best Q given its choice for S.

20 The prime symbol (′) denotes a first derivative; here, the first derivative is with respect to S.

21 The double-prime symbol (″) denotes a second derivative.

22 By optimal level of use, I mean the scope of activities that benefit from the measurement standard. A measurement standard is fixed in the sense that it is either used or not used.

23 … as economic theory would predict.

3 Public support of measurement standards

Market failure

Bator, in his seminal 1958 article, "The Anatomy of Market Failure," defines the term *market failure* in the following way (p. 351):

> Typically, at least in allocation theory, we mean the failure of a more or less idealized system of price-market institutions to sustain "desirable" activities or to estop "undesirable" activities. The desirability of an activity, in turn, is evaluated relative to the solution values of some explicit or implied maximum-welfare problem.

And, as Bator noted in a footnote in his article, the word *activities* (in the quoted passage above) is intended to refer to both consumption as well as production. As a result of market failure, or more precisely as a result of the barriers that bring about a market failure, neither consumers nor producers will invest the socially desirable amount in measurement science (i.e., in the underlying research or in the actual development process) because neither will have the ability to appropriate fully all of the benefits from their development of a measurement standard.[1]

A more specific reference about the implications of market failure for the development of a measurement standard was offered by Swann (2009). He presented three arguments for public support of a nation's system of measurement—a national measurement infrastructure—including public sector funded research focused on metrology (Swann, 2009, p. v):[2]

> Economists recognise three particular properties of [measurement infrastructures]. First, they are subject to important economies of scale and scope. Second, they are public goods. And third, the private sector left to its own devices would tend to under-invest in [measurement

DOI: 10.4324/9781003186953-3

infrastructures], so that government support and co-ordination is required.

National metrology laboratories are measurement infrastructures that are active in many countries as discussed in Chapter 4. In the United States, NIST is the national metrology laboratory, and it has the following mission:[3]

> To promote U.S. innovation and industrial competitiveness by advancing measurement science, standards, and technology in ways that enhance economic security and improve our quality of life.

And, NIST's core competencies for meeting this mission are measurement science, rigorous traceability, and the development and use of standards.

A brief history of the National Institute of Standards and Technology (NIST)[4]

The concept of the U.S. public sector's involvement in measurement standards traces to the Articles of Confederation signed on July 9, 1778.[5] Therein it is stated:

> The United States, in Congress assembled, shall also have the sole and exclusive right and power of regulating the alloy and value of coin struck by their own authority or by that of the respective States; fixing the standard of weights and measures throughout the United States.

This responsibility of fixing "the standard of weights and measures" was repeated in Article 1 of the Constitution of the United States:

> The Congress shall have power … To coin money, regulate the value thereof, and of foreign coin, and fix the standard of weights and measures.

The responsibility for the construction and distribution of weights and measures was initially assigned to the Secretary of the Treasury through a joint resolution on June 14, 1836:

> That the Secretary of the Treasury be, and he hereby is directed to cause a complete set of all the weights and measures adopted as standards, and now either made or in the progress of manufacture for the use of

> the several custom-houses, and for other purposes, to be delivered to the Governor of each State in the Union, or such person as he may appoint, for the use of the State respectively, to the end that an uniform standard of weights and measures may be established throughout the United States.

President Andrew Johnson authorized the use of the metric system in the United States on July 28, 1866, through An Act to Authorize the Use of the Metric System of Weights and Measures:

> Be it enacted … [t]hat from and after the passage of this act it shall be lawful throughout the United States of America to employ the weights and measures of the metric system; and no contract or dealing, or pleading in any court, shall be deemed invalid or liable to objection because the weights or measures expressed or referred to therein are weights and measures of the metric system … And be it further enacted, That the tables in the schedule hereto annexed shall be recognized in the construction of contracts, and in all legal proceedings, as establishing, in terms of the weights and measures expressed therein in terms of the metric system; and said tables may be lawfully used for computing, determining, and expressing in customary weights and measures the weights and measures of the metric system.

The French government held an international conference in 1872, which included the participation of the United States, to settle on procedures for the preparation of prototype metric standards in response to growing interest in the use of the metric system in scientific research.[6] Then, on May 20, 1875, the United States participated in the Convention of the Meter in Paris and was one of the eighteen signatory nations to the Treaty of the Meter.[7] Following this event, in a Joint Resolution before Congress on March 3, 1881, it was resolved that:

> The Secretary of the Treasury be, and he is hereby directed to cause a complete set of all the weights and measures adopted as standards to be delivered to the governor of each State in the Union, for the use of agricultural colleges in the States, respectively, which have received a grant of lands from the United States, and also one set of the same for the use of the Smithsonian Institution.

Then, the Act of 11 July 1890, gave authority to the Office of Construction of Standard Weights and Measures (or Office of Standard Weights and

Measures), which had been established in 1836 within the Treasury's Coast and Geodetic Survey office:

> For construction and verification of standard weights and measures, including metric standards, for the custom-houses, and other offices of the United States, and for the several States.

Following a long history of U.S. leaders calling for uniformity in science, traceable at least to the several formal proposals for the establishment of a Department of Science in the early 1880s, and coupled with the growing inability of the Office of Weights and Measures to handle the explosion of arbitrary standards in all aspects of federal and state activity, it was inevitable that a standards laboratory would need to be established. The political force for this laboratory came in 1900 through Lyman Gage, then Secretary of the Treasury under President William McKinley. It was Gage who championed a national standards laboratory. His efforts were instrumental in the passage of the March 3, 1901, Act (Public Law 177-56), often referred to as the Organic Act of 1901. With regard to the Office of Standard Weights and Measures, to be renamed the National Bureau of Standards (NBS), within the Department of the Treasury, the Organic Act states:

> That the functions of the [B]ureau shall consist in the custody of the standards; the comparison of the standards used in scientific investigations, engineering, manufacturing, commerce, and educational institutions with the standards adopted or recognized by the Government; the construction, when necessary, of standards, their multiples and subdivisions; the testing and calibration of standard measuring apparatus; the solution of problems which arise in connection with standards; the determination of physical constants and the properties of materials, when such data are of great importance to scientific or manufacturing interests and are not to be obtained of sufficient accuracy elsewhere.

The Organic Act of 1901 and the activities of the Bureau might reasonably be viewed as the first national effort in the United States to legislate the transfer of technology in the form of technical knowledge, or in some instances a technical artifact, from the public sector to all sectors in the economy.

In late 1901, the Bureau was transferred from the Department of the Treasury to the Department of Commerce and Labor, the latter which had been established under the Act of 14 February 1903. Initially, more than one-half of the testing at the Bureau was for government use rather than for the use of enhancing commerce. For example, according to Cochrane (1966, p. 91), as early as 1906:

> there was a wave of reform going on all through the Government service as to proper specifications and proper tests to determine whether goods purchased [by the Government] complied with specification.

The products tested at the Bureau ranged from light bulbs to the tensile strength of elevator cables. As more and more products were tested and then rejected by the Bureau's tests, manufacturers began to interact with the Bureau "for advice and help with their materials, measuring, and testing apparatus, and methods of quality control" (Cochrane, 1966, p. 92). Then, in 1913, when the Department of Labor was established as a separate administrative entity, the Bureau formally became administratively part of the Department of Commerce.

World War I brought about an understanding for the need for standardization across agencies that purchased goods that are supply chain related. Thus, the transfer of technology—tacit technical knowledge in the form of know-how as well as codified practices—from the public sector's Bureau to private sector manufacturers had begun, and this transfer activity increased exponentially during the first decade of the Bureau's life (Cochrane, 1966).

After World War I, then Secretary of Commerce Herbert Hoover initiated an industrial survey for the purpose of identifying wasteful practices in industry. The industrial survey concluded that as much as 25 percent of production costs could be eliminated without affecting quality (Cochrane, 1966). This finding motivated a wider role for standardization, and this thinking was later exacerbated by the spread of assembly line production to more efficient use of economic inputs. Yet again, the Bureau's technical knowledge was being transferred to industry and eventually to consumers.

However, during World War II, the role of the Bureau expanded to focus on the development and improvement of military technology. And, by the end of World War II, there was the view that the federal government, through the expertise of the Bureau, should be responsible for basic research—the discovery of new knowledge—rather than applied industrial research.

In 1953, Secretary of Commerce Sinclair Weeks asked the National Academy of Sciences to "convene an *ad hoc* committee to evaluate the function and operations of the NBS in relation to the current national needs" (Cochrane, 1966, p. 495). Perhaps most relevant, from a technology transfer to the private sector perspective was the recommendation from the Academy's *ad hoc* committee that the weapons programs at the NBS be transferred to the Department of Defense. The *ad hoc* committee recommended that the Bureau be restored to its "essential services for our industrial society" (Cochrane, 1966, p. 496). The *ad hoc* committee also offered a recommendation for the modernization of the Bureau's facilities which were "in a sordid mess" (Cochrane, 1996, p. 503). After much debate and planning, ground was broken on June 14, 1961, on a 550-acre plot of land in Gaithersburg, Maryland. The Gaithersburg campus was formally dedicated in 1966.

As Schooley (2000, p. 646) suggested:

> Given the increased emphasis on international competitiveness, technology transfer, and industrial productivity in the dialog between NBS and Congress during the 1980s, new legislation to re-define the mission of the Bureau was almost a certainty. The change in the name of the agency—in the view of the Congress—merely served to underscore its new role within the Department of Commerce.

It was a well-known fact by the mid- to late 1970s that many U.S. industries were faltering in terms of their technological advances. For example, total factor productivity (TFP) is widely regarded as an index of technological advancement within an economy. Much has been written about the culprits for the so-called productivity slowdown (e.g., Link and Siegel, 2003; Leyden and Link, 2015), but most scholars point to declining investments in R&D as a cause of a slowdown in technological advancements, which, in turn, was holding down productivity growth. Causation aside, one consequence of these periods of slowdown was a decline in the international competitiveness of many U.S. industries.[8]

In fact, the Technology Administration within the Department of Commerce reported trends, based on data and information relative to the mid- to late 1980s, in several emerging technologies in which the United States was losing, and in some instances losing badly, to Japan in particular (USDOC, 1990, p. 13):

> The United States was losing in terms of trends in R&D investments in advanced materials, biotechnology, digital imaging technology, sensor technology, and superconductors.
>
> The United States was losing in terms of trends in new product introductions in advanced materials, advanced semiconductor devices, high-density data storage, high-performance computing, medical devices and diagnostics (including digital imaging technology), optoelectronics, and superconductors.

In the mid-1980s, Congress considered "several initiatives to improve American competitiveness in world-wide markets" (Schooley, 2000, p. 613). These considerations were finally codified in the Omnibus Trade and Completeness Act of 1988 (Public Law 100-418). Stated therein:[9]

> The National Bureau of Standards since its establishment has served as the Federal focal point in developing basic measurement standards and related technologies, has taken a lead role in stimulating cooperative work among private industrial organizations in efforts to surmount technological hurdles, and otherwise has been responsible for assisting in the improvement of industrial technology ... It is the purpose of this Act to rename the National Bureau of Standards as the National Institute of Standards and Technology [NIST] and to modernize and restructure that agency to augment its unique ability *to enhance the competitiveness of American industry* [emphasis added] ... The Secretary of Commerce ... acting through the Director of the Institute ... and, if appropriate, through other officials, is authorized to take all actions necessary and appropriate to accomplish the purposes of this Act, including the following functions of the Institute ... to invent, develop, and (when appropriate) promote *transfer to the private sector* [emphasis added] of measurement devices to serve special national needs ... to demonstrate the results of the Institute's activities by exhibits or other *methods of technology transfer* [emphasis added], including the use of scientific or technical personnel of the Institute for part-time or intermittent teaching and training activities at educational institutions of higher learning as part of and incidental to their official duties.

NIST: One of many national metrology laboratories

Table 3.1 is perhaps the most complete global listing and description of country by country national metrology laboratories and their missions. The table is presented here as a reference source, and it will not be discussed in detail in this book except to note the public sector's emphasis on measurement standards is global. Some countries have more than one public sector organization that is responsible to the development and maintenance of measurement standards. When identifiable, all such organizations are listed in Table 3.1.[10]

Metrology conducted at NIST and measurement standards developed at NIST based on underlying measurement science are discussed in detail in Chapter 4.

Table 3.1 Description of national metrology laboratories, by country

Country (alphabetical)	*Laboratory*	*Mission statement / priority statement (quoted or translated)*
Albania	Drejtoria e Përgjithshme e Metrologjisë (DPM; In English, "General Directorate of Metrology") www.dpm.gov.al/en/	Maintain and use the national units of measurement; to protect consumers by organizing control of measuring instruments in the fields of official and commercial transactions, health protection, environment and technical security, as well as quantitative control of pre-packages; provide calibration services to manufacturers and users of metering tools to be competitive in the domestic and overseas market. www.dpm.gov.al/en/rreth-nesh/
Antigua	Antigua and Barbuda Bureau of Standards https://abbs.gov.ag/	To provide the best possible technical assistance for the economic and industrial development of Antigua and Barbuda, through the preparation and promulgation of standards, and in so doing become a proactive catalyst for consumer protection by ensuring that minimum standards exist for all goods, services and the environment. https://abbs.gov.ag/the-bureau/about-abbs/
Argentina	Instituto Nacional de Tecnología Industrial (INTI) www.inti.gov.ar/	Strengthen industrial competitiveness throughout the country through technology transfer, compliance with metrological legislation and the promotion of technological development, and innovation in all productive sectors. www.inti.gob.ar/conoces-al-inti
Australia	National Measurement Institute www.measurement.gov.au/	To lead and coordinate Australia's measurement system; ensure Australia's measurement system is trusted; enhance trade, investment, and economic growth; deliver critical measurement services; and evolve capability to serve key economic sectors. www.industry.gov.au/about-us/our-structure/about-the-national-measurement-institute

(*Continued*)

Table 3.1 (Continued) Description of national metrology laboratories, by country

Country (alphabetical)	*Laboratory*	*Mission statement / priority statement (quoted or translated)*
Austria	BEV – Federal Office of Metrology and Surveying www.bev.gv.at/	We are a public institution run by modern management methods with a long tradition. We offer products and services of the highest quality in Germany and abroad, both in the sovereign and partially legal area. In addition to central specialist and administrative facilities, we have a dense network of regional offices and constantly optimized telecommunications connections. We are there for our customers. That is why we offer you our wide range of products and services for testing and verification services, surveying services, geographic information, and cartography as well as our know-how for interdisciplinary issues across the whole of Germany. Customer orientation, customer proximity and flexibility are just as much a part of our success factors as the guaranteed objectivity and reliability. Thanks to our numerous independent experts and highly trained employees, we are able to solve complex problems. Our employees are our greatest asset. That is why we create optimal organizational structures for them that motivate the individual to high performance and personal responsibility. Lived partnership, participation and consistent subsidiarity internally and externally secure our common values such as security, openness, and satisfaction. Our activities are geared towards maximum efficiency. Constant optimization of the organization and its permanent orientation to the quality requirements is just as natural for us as it is for our partners. We are in the service of Austria and its citizens. As a reliable partner of the Austrian economy and all consumers, we guarantee that national calibration standards are always available and, based on our extensive databases, provide ground-related data bases for all of Austria. This is how we guarantee legal certainty. www.bev.gv.at/portal/page?_pageid=713,2609350&_dad=portal&_schema=PORTAL

Azerbaijan	Azerbaijan Institute of Standardization (AZSTAND) http://azstand.gov.az/az	The aim is to bring the country's national standardization system in line with international requirements, increase product safety, quality, competitiveness, and export potential. http://azstand.gov.az/az/page/22
Bahamas	Bahamas Bureau of Standards and Quality https://www.bbsq.bs/en/	Advance national development through the facilitation and promotion of quality services in standardization, metrology, and conformity assessment to protect the consumer, enhance international trade and competitiveness of goods and services. www.bbsq.bs/en/about-bbsq
Barbados	Barbados National Standards Institution www.commonwealthofnations.org/sectors-barbados/government/national_agencies/	To regulate and ensure that international standards are maintained. www.commonwealthofnations.org/sectors-barbados/government/national_agencies/
Belgium	Ministry of Economic Affairs https://economie.fgov.be/nl	To create the conditions for a competitive, sustainable, and balanced operation of the goods and services market in Belgium. In this respect, the FPS Economy wants to know the goods and services market thoroughly and to support them well in order to stimulate them better. https://economie.fgov.be/nl/over-de-fod/missie-visie-waarden/missie
Belize	Bureau of Standards http://bbs.gov.bz/	To facilitate, promote and encourage the use of quality services in Metrology, Standardization and Conformity Assessment thereby contributing to competitiveness of goods and services, facilitation of trade and the protection of consumers. http://bbs.gov.bz/vision-and-mission/

(*Continued*)

Table 3.1 (Continued) Description of national metrology laboratories, by country

Country (alphabetical)	*Laboratory*	*Mission statement / priority statement (quoted or translated)*
Bolivia	Bolivian Institute of Metrology (IBMETRO) www.ibmetro.gob.bo/web/	Guarding national measurement standards to provide services that promote accuracy and quality, generating confidence in the productive sector and the consumer society. www.ibmetro.gob.bo/web/mision_vision
Brazil	Instituto Nacional de Metrologia, Normalização e Qualidade Industrial (INMETRO) www.inmetro.gov.br/english/	The right measure to promote confidence in society and competitiveness in the productive sector. www4.inmetro.gov.br/index.php/acesso-a-informacao/institucional
Canada	National Research Council Canada www.nrc-cnrc.gc.ca/eng/index.html	To have an impact by advancing knowledge, applying leading-edge technologies, and working with other innovators to find creative, relevant, and sustainable solutions to Canada's current and future economic, social, and environmental challenges. https://nrc.canada.ca/en/corporate/about-nrc
Chile	Instituo Nacional de Normalización (INN) www.inn.cl/	Contribute to society with quality assurance and improvement, through the development of technical standards, conformity assessment accreditation, the coordination of the National Metrology Network and the transfer of knowledge, to increase the added value of the various productive sectors and improve people's quality of life, with emphasis on those sectors prioritized by public policies, with excellence and technical independence. www.inn.cl/quienes-somos

China	National Institute of Metrology http://en.nim.ac.cn/	NIM has thoroughly implemented the scientific concept of development, adheres to the principle of independent innovation, major breakthroughs, supporting development and leading the future; and is committed to support the country's economic and social development as the starting point and the foothold of the development of measurement technology; persist in strengthening the frontier research of fundamental metrology, serving the national strategic objectives and improving the three strategic tasks of measurement, calibration and service capabilities; persist in taking the construction of new areas of metrological science and technology as the main direction of national strategic emerging industries for the country to speed up the transformation of the mode of economic development and to develop biosafety, energy, health, new materials, nano-tech, the environment, quality of life and a new generation of information technology. NIM regards optimizing the professional structure, strengthening the basic construction, focusing on scientific and technological cooperation, cultivating backbone talents and creating a policy environment as the important focus of measuring scientific and technological innovation and sustainable development; NIM continues to make progress in order to establish world leading measurement and scientific research institutions, and achieve more accomplishments and train more talents. https://en.nim.ac.cn/nim/introduction
Colombia	Superintendencia de Industria y Comercio, SIC www.sic.gov.co/	The Superintendency of Industry and Commerce watches over the good functioning of the markets by monitoring and protecting free economic competition, consumer rights, compliance with aspects related to legal metrology and technical regulations, the valuation activity of the country, and the management of the Chambers of Commerce. At the same time, it is responsible for the protection of personal data, manages and promotes the Industrial Property System and settles disputes that arise in the event of affectations of particular rights related to consumer protection, unfair competition matters and industrial property rights. This is achieved thanks to the commitment and technical competence of its human talent, which, coupled with physical, technological, and financial resources, contributes to the development of business activity and the protection of consumer rights in Colombia. www.sic.gov.co/mision-y-vision

(*Continued*)

Table 3.1 (Continued) Description of national metrology laboratories, by country

Country (alphabetical)	*Laboratory*	*Mission statement / priority statement (quoted or translated)*
Costa Rica	Ministerio de Industria y Commercio www.meic.go.cr/	We are the national body that fosters and supports economic and social development through policies that facilitate the strengthening of the competitiveness of the industry, commerce and services sectors, especially micro, small and medium-sized enterprises (SMEs), promoting productive chains, improving state capacity to manage trade, ensuring fair competition, regulatory improvement, quality and consumer support. www.meic.go.cr/meic/web/82/meic/mision.php
Czech Republic	Czech Metrological Institute www.cmi.cz/?language=en	Fulfillment of the activities in administration for the field of metrology according to Law about metrology Nr. 505/90 Sb. www.cmi.cz/About%20CMI?language=en
Denmark	Danish Institute of Fundamental Metrology (DFM)https://dfm-metrology.com/	To develop and disseminate measurement knowledge at an international level with focus on Danish interests. https://dfm-metrology.com/dfms-mission/
Dominica	Dominica Bureau of Standards (DBOS) www.dominicastandards.org/	The Dominica Bureau of Standards develops, establishes, maintains and promotes standards for improving industrial development, industrial efficiency, promoting the health and safety of consumers as well as protecting the environment, food and food products, the quality of life for the citizenry and the facilitation of trade. https://website.crosq.org/index.php/dominica
Dominican Republic	Dominican System for Quality (SIDOCAL) www.indocal.gob.do/	Develop standardization and metrology by providing conformity assessment services, supported by international good practices, with an increasingly trained staff, to achieve productive competitiveness and the well-being of all Dominican citizens. www.indocal.gob.do/sobre-nosotros/quienes-somos/
Ecuador	Instituto Ecuatoriano de Normalizacion (INEN) www.normalizacion.gob.ec/	Strengthen the Ecuadorian Quality System, contributing to the competitiveness, trust and satisfaction of the interested parties, through the continuous improvement of the standardization, technical regulation, conformity assessment and metrology processes, with our competent human talent and complying with the legal and regulatory requirements. www.normalizacion.gob.ec/mision-y-valores-institucionales/

Egypt	National Institute for Standards (NIS) www.nis.sci.eg/	Developed and maintained the nation's primary measurement standards and disseminated them to the end user with the highest possible accuracy. These primary standards underpin an infrastructure of traceability through Egypt and the world to ensure accuracy and consistency of measurements. www.linkedin.com/company/nis-national-institute-for-standards-of-egypt/about/
El Salvador	Consejo Nacional de Ciencia y Technología (CONACYT) www.conacyt.gob.sv/	The New CONACYT is a state implementing and executing entity for national policies in the field of scientific and technological development and support for the promotion of innovation, which promotes professional training, stimulates research and the adoption of new technologies, and disseminates scientific knowledge. and technological, so that it is the base of the social, economic, and environmental development, that leads to improving the quality of life of the Salvadoran population. www.conacyt.gob.sv/?page_id=161
Finland	Centre for Metrology (MIKES or VTT MIKES) www.mikes.fi/en/	Responsible for the implementation and development of the national measurement standards system and realization of the SI units in Finland. www.mikes.fi/en/about-us
Finland	Finnish Standards Association www.sfs.fi/en/	The purpose of the Association is to function as the central body for standardization in Finland and to maintain and promote the application of standards and functions relating or supporting standardization according to the needs of Finnish society and by due consideration to international requirements. The purpose of the Association is not the attaining of direct financial benefit for those who participate. www.sfs.fi/files/8885/SFS_saannot_EN_web.pdf
France	Laboratoire National d'Essais www.lne.fr/	To guide not only companies, in their strategies aimed at enhancing competitiveness and innovation, but also to steer Society at large towards more sustainable and secure development. www.lne.fr/en/about-us/missions
Germany	Physikalisch-Technische Bundesanstalt (PTB) www.ptb.de/index_en.html	To ensure a continuously functioning and, consequently, a reliable and progressive metrological infrastructure which meets both the highest requirements of science and high-tech industry, on the one hand, and the marginal conditions of legal metrology in everyday life, on the other hand. www.ptb.de/cms/en/about-us-careers/about-us/ptbs-tasks.html

(Continued)

Table 3.1 (Continued) Description of national metrology laboratories, by country

Country (alphabetical)	*Laboratory*	*Mission statement / priority statement (quoted or translated)*
Germany	Federal Institute for Materials Research and Testing (BAM) www.bam.de/index_en.htm	Ensure safety in technology and chemistry. www.bam.de/Navigation/EN/About-us/Our-Mission-Statement/our-mission-statement.html
Ghana	Ghana Standards Board www.gsa.gov.gh/	To contribute towards the growth of industry, protect consumers and facilitate trade through standardization, metrology, and conformity assessment. www.gsa.gov.gh/about/
Grenada	Grenada Bureau of Standards http://gdbs.gd/	Improving the quality competitiveness of Grenadian Industries thus enhancing the quality of life of Grenadians through standardization. http://gdbs.gd/About-Us.html
Greece	Hellenic Institute of Metrology (EIM) www.eim.gr/language/en/	With its modern infrastructure, state of the art technology and expert know-how, EIM develops activities, promotes co-operations, and provides services, which contribute to the growth of a competitive national economy. Its activities contribute to the quality of products and services, the improvement of methods and processes in manufacturing and production, as well as the assurance of fair trade and consumer safety & protection. www.eim.gr/the-identity-of-eim/
Guatemala	Comisión Guatemalteca de Normas www.mineco.gob.gt/	The Guatemalan Standards Commission – COGUANOR – is the nationally and internationally recognized entity, which manages technical standardization and related activities, to promote the obtaining of quality products and services, helping to improve competitiveness and quality of life, as well as build trust among the sectors involved. www.coguanor.gob.gt/index.php?id=7
Guyana	Guyana National Bureau of Standards www.gnbsgy.org/	To develop and implement the National Quality Infrastructure in partnership with key stakeholders towards sustainable socio-economic development and consumer protection. https://gnbsgy.org/about-us/
Haiti	Ministry of Commerce and Industry www.iso.org/member/5304435.html	To organize and manage activities related to standardization, certification, industrial metrology, promotion of quality and to provide technical support for all efforts undertaken in pursuit of these objectives. www.iso.org/member/5304435.html

Honduras	Departamento de Ingeniería Química Universidad www.unah.hn/	We are a State and Autonomous University; Constitutionally responsible for organizing, directing, and developing the third and fourth levels of the national educational system. Our field of scientific production and action is universal. Our commitment is to contribute through the training of professionals, research and the University-Society link to the sustainable human development of the country and through the science and culture that we generate, to contribute to all of Honduras participating in universality and to develop in conditions of equity and humanism. Addressing the academic relevance for the diverse regional and national needs. https://ingenieria.unah.edu.hn/facultad/vision-and-mision
Hungary	Metrology and Technical Supervisory Department https://mkeh.gov.hu/meresugy	[no specific mission statement]
Iceland	Consumer Agency (Metrology Division) www.neytendastofa.is/english/the-consumer-agency/	To ensure that measurements in Iceland fulfil international requirements and to ensure that the International System of Units (SI) is used in Iceland. www.neytendastofa.is/english/metrology-division/
India	National Physical Laboratory (NPL) www.nplindia.org/	The main aim of the laboratory is to strengthen and advance physics-based research and development for the overall development of science and technology in the country. www.nplindia.in/npl-charter
Indonesia	Research and Development Center for Calibration, Instrumentation and Metrology (KIM-LIPI) www.metrologi.lipi.go.id/	[no specific mission statement]
Ireland	National Metrology Lab (NML) www.nsai.ie/national-metrology/	[no specific mission statement]
Ireland	National Standards Authority of Ireland www.nsai.ie/	To inspire consumer confidence and create the infrastructure for products and services to be recognized and relied on, all over the world. www.nsai.ie/about/

(Continued)

Table 3.1 (Continued) Description of national metrology laboratories, by country

Country (alphabetical)	*Laboratory*	*Mission statement / priority statement (quoted or translated)*
Israel	National Physical Laboratory www.gov.il/en/Departments/Units/national_physics_laboratory	Calibrating equipment used by calibration and inspection labs that serve Israel's industries and trade; comparing Israeli measurement standards with those used in countries that have signed the Meter Convention in order to ensure consistency; developing new standards, such as systems that measure acidity and conductivity in solutions, etc.; comparing various forms of measurement, calibration and inspection in laboratories in Israel; serving as the exclusive representative of the State of Israel in the international BIPM organization, responsible for implementing the Meter Convention. Also active in other national and international organizations responsible for measurements, calibration, and inspections. www.gov.il/en/Departments/Units/national_physics_laboratory)
Italy	Istituto Nazionale di Ricerca Metrologica www.inrim.eu/	INRIM is a public research center and is Italy's national metrology institute (NMI). INRIM realizes, maintains, and develops the national reference standards of the measurement units of the International System (SI), consisting of seven base units – meter, kilogram, second, ampere, kelvin, mole, and candela – and derived units. Thanks to these standards, the Institute ensures measurements that are reliable and comparable on both a national and international scale. INRIM's research spans many other areas such as materials science, nanoscience, quantum optics, studies on the fundamental constants of physics. Basic and applied research and the development of new measurement technologies and instruments enhance the metrology activity. Through seminars, exhibitions, events, and conferences, INRIM presents and disseminates its scientific findings and advancements. The Institute promotes education and training for young scientists organizing PhD courses and financing scholarships and research grants. To meet the needs of industry, INRIM has a dedicated department working in close contact with the world of production and providing consultancy, calibration, and testing services. The Institute supports the National Laboratory Accreditation System by ensuring the quality of measurement standards and procedures and promoting the dissemination

Italy	Istituto Nazionale di Metrologia delle Radiaziono Ionizzanti Roma (ENEA) www.enea.it/en/home-luglio-2015?set_language=en&cl=en	ENEA is the National Agency for New Technologies, Energy and Sustainable Economic Development, a public body aimed at research, technological innovation and the provision of advanced services to enterprises, public administration and citizens in the sectors of energy, the environment and sustainable economic development. www.enea.it/en/enea/about-us
Italy	Consiglio Nazionale delle Ricerche (CNR) www.cnr.it/sitocnr/home.html	Carrying out research projects, promoting innovation and competitiveness of the national industrial system, the internationalization of the national research system, and of providing technologies and solutions to emerging needs in the public and private sector. www.cnr.it/it/chi-siamo
Jamaica	Bureau of Standards Jamaica www.bsj.org.jm/	The Bureau of Standards Jamaica is a customer-focused organization that promotes international competitiveness of Jamaican producers, facilitates business development and trade, and supports consumer protection by providing standardization, metrology, testing, certification, and training services through visionary leadership, consultants, teamwork, and a committed, motivated workforce. www.bsj.org.jm/mission-mandate-vision
Japan	National Institute of Advanced Industrial Science and Technology (AIST) www.aist.go.jp/index_en.html	To develop science and technology that complements society and the environment. www.aist.go.jp/aist_e/about_aist/charter/charter.html
Jordan	Jordan Standards and Metrology www.jsmo.gov.jo/en/Pages/default.aspx	Adopt of a national system for standardization and metrology based on accepted international practices; keep pace with scientific and technical developments in the fields of standards, metrology, conformity assessment and laboratory accreditation; ensure the health and safety of the Kingdom's citizenry and protection of the environment by making sure that goods, products and services are in compliance with the technical regulations adopted by the Organization for the purpose; and ensure the quality of local goods, products and services through the adoption of appropriate Jordanian Standards in order to enhance their competitiveness in the local and international markets and thus support the national economy. www.jsmo.gov.jo/en/About/Pages/default.aspx

(Continued)

Table 3.1 (Continued) Description of national metrology laboratories, by country

Country (alphabetical)	*Laboratory*	*Mission statement / priority statement (quoted or translated)*
Kazakstan	Kazakhstan Institute of Metrology https://kazinmetr.kz/eng/	Achievement of international reliance to accuracy and reliability of measurements in Kazakhstan, formation of a regulatory system in compliance with international requirements, conduction of highly precise measurements for industry, research engineering, establishment of regional center for providing metrological service for industries. https://kazinmetr.kz/eng/about/
Kenya	Weights and Measures Office www.industrialization.go.ke/index.php/departments/state-department-of-trade/430-department-of-weights-measures	The Mission of the Weights and Measures Department is to facilitate fair trade by ensuring use of accurate weighing and measuring equipment, promoting fair business practices, and protecting the consumer against exploitation in the sale of goods and services. www.industrialization.go.ke/index.php/departments/state-department-of-trade/430-department-of-weights-measures
Kenya	Kenya Burau of Standards www.kebs.org/	To provide standards based solutions that promote innovation, trade, and quality of life. www.kebs.org/index.php?option=com_content&view=article&id=57&Itemid=257
Republic of Korea	Korea Research Institute of Standards and Science (KRISS) www.kriss.re.kr/	Establishment, maintenance, and improvement of national measurement standards (representative organizations of national measurement standards). www.kriss.re.kr/introduce/view.do?pg=mission_function
Kurgyzstan	Center for Standardization and Metrology at the Ministry of Economics of the Kyrgyz Republic http://mineconom.gov.kg/ru/ministry/structure	[no specific mission statement]

Lithuania	Center for Physical Sciences and Technology (Department of Metrology) www.ftmc.lt/department-of-metrology	Maintains and develops national standards realizing the units of measurement in the following metrology areas: thermometry; time and frequency; electricity and magnetism; amount of substance; ionizing radiation. Ensures traceability of the unit values realized to the International system of units SI; by performing measurements and calibrations, disseminates the values to the scientific and state establishments as well as industry of Lithuania; transmits the value of exact time via internet to any user requesting it for free. www.ftmc.lt/department-of-metrology)
Luxembourg	Luxembourg Institute for Standardization, Accreditation, Safety and Quality of Products and Services (ILNAS) https://portail-qualite.public.lu/fr.html	Standardization, accreditation and notification, digital confidence, market surveillance, and metrology. https://portail-qualite.public.lu/fr/acteurs/ilnas.html
Malaysia	Standards and Industrial Research Institute of Malaysia (SIRIM) www.sirim.my/	[no specific mission statement]
Malta	Malta Competition and Consumer Affairs Authority (MCCAA) https://mccaa.org.mt/	To promote and enhance competition; to safeguard consumers' interests and enhance their welfare; to promote voluntary standards and provide standardization related services; to promote the national metrology strategy; to promote the smooth transposition and adoption of technical regulations; and to perform such other function that may be assigned to it under this or any other law or regulations. https://mccaa.org.mt/Section/Content?contentId=1272
Mauritius	Mauritius Standards Bureau http://msb.intnet.mu/English/Pages/default.aspx	To spearhead industrial development and the economic growth of Mauritius through the timely delivery of Metrology, Standards, Testing and Quality Assurance (MSTQ) services. http://msb.intnet.mu/English/AboutUs/Pages/About-MSB.aspx

(*Continued*)

Table 3.1 (Continued) Description of national metrology laboratories, by country

Country (alphabetical)	*Laboratory*	*Mission statement / priority statement (quoted or translated)*
Mexico	Centro Nacional de Metrología (CENAM) www.cenam.mx/	Institution of the Mexican State leader in the science of measurements, with competent, committed, and honest staff. It offers innovative services and solutions based on scientific knowledge and technological development and has a positive impact on trade, industrial competitiveness, the environment, and the well-being of the population, with equity and transparency. It is responsible for establishing and maintaining national standards, offering metrological services such as calibration of instruments and standards, certification and development of reference materials, specialized courses in metrology, proficiency testing and consulting. It maintains close contact with other national laboratories and with international organizations related to metrology, in order to ensure international recognition of Mexico's national standards and, consequently, to promote acceptance of the products and services of our country. CENAM, being the primary laboratory in Mexico, does not carry out regulatory activities. The Federal Law on Metrology and Standardization and its Regulations establish the responsibility of the Ministry of Economy and other organizations, such as the National Commission for Standardization and the Federal Consumer Protection Agency, to apply the provisions established by law. www.gob.mx/cenam/que-hacemos
Moldova	Department of Standardization and Metrology of the Republic of Moldova www.standard.md/?l=en	To contribute to increasing economic competitiveness, sustainable growth and welfare enhancing sustainable use of resources. www.standard.md/tabview.php?l=en&idc=149&t=/About-ISM/Mission-vision-and-values-ISM

Mongolia	Mongolian National Centre for Standardization and Metrology https://masm.gov.mn/masmj/	In line with Mongolia's development strategy and trends, the aim is to ensure national, social, and economic security, increase exports, and support the development of national industries through standardization, metrology, conformity assessment, and sampling control policies. https://masm.gov.mn/masmj/байгууллагын-товч-танилцуулга/
Nepal	Nepal Bureau of Standards and Metrology http://nbsm.gov.np/	[no specific mission statement]
Netherlands	Nederlands Meetinstituut (MNi) www.nmi.nl/	[no specific mission statement]
New Zealand	Measurement Standards Laboratory www.measurement.govt.nz/	To accelerate New Zealand's economic growth and enhance well-being through access to world-class measurement standards and advice. www.measurement.govt.nz/about-us/
Nicaragua	Ministerio de Fomento, Industria, y Comercio www.mific.gob.ni/	Formulate policies, regulations, programs, and strategies that regulate and boost national trade, facilitate exports, and strengthen the industrial sector, contributing to the country's economic development. www.mific.gob.ni/QuienesSomos
Norway	Justervesenet (Norwegian Metrology Service) www.justervesenet.no/en/	Responsible for the Norwegian metrology infrastructure and for ensuring its national and international acceptance. www.justervesenet.no/en/

(*Continued*)

Table 3.1 (Continued) Description of national metrology laboratories, by country

Country (alphabetical)	*Laboratory*	*Mission statement / priority statement (quoted or translated)*
Pakistan	Pakistan Standards and Quality Control Authority (PSQCA)http://updated.psqca.com.pk/	To foster and promote standards and conformity assessment as a means of advancing the national economy, promoting industrial efficiency and development, ensuring the health and safety of the public, protecting the consumers. Facilitating domestic and international trade and furthering international co-operation relation to Standards and conformity assessment in the interest of consumers. http://updated.psqca.com.pk/about-us/
Pakistan	National Physical Standards Laboratory http://pcsir.gov.pk/?pg=10203	To re-align PCSIR as a cost-effective technology solution provider for public and private sectors, especially for SMEs. http://pcsir.gov.pk/?pg=10231
Panama	Ministerio de Comercio e Industrias www.mici.gob.pa/	Planning, organization, coordination, direction, and control of activities aimed at making possible the creation, development and expansion of trade, industry, financial activities, research and use of mineral resources in the country, and compliance with the policy. foreign trade. https://mici.gob.pa/quienes-somos/vision-mision-logo
Panama	Centro Nacional de Metrologia de Panamá (CENAMEP) www.cenamep.org.pa/	Define, maintain, and disseminate national measurement standards and Metrological knowledge, to help guarantee the safety and quality of life of people, protect the environment, and ensure innovation and competitiveness in the country. www.cenamep.org.pa/mision-y-vision/
Panama	Secretaría Nacional de Ciencia y Tecnología (SENACYT) www.senacyt.gob.pa/	Convert science and technology into sustainable development tools for Panama. www.senacyt.gob.pa/sobre-nosotros/
Paraguay	Instituto Nacional de Tecnología y Normalización (INTN) www.intn.gov.py/	Contribute to society, industry, commerce, the productive sector, through research, technical assistance services, standardization, metrology, electrical safety, certification and inspection, to improve the quality of products, services, well-being and safety of people, with a focus on social and environmental responsibility. www.intn.gov.py/index.php/institucion/mision-y-vision

Peru	Servicio Nacional de Metrologia www.indecopi.gob.pe/	Defend, promote, and strengthen competition in markets, creativity and innovation and balance in consumer relations, in favor of the well-being of citizens, in a transparent, solid, predictable way and in harmony with business freedom. www.indecopi.gob.pe/mision
Philippines	National Metrology Laboratory (NMLPHIL) http://nml.gov.ph/	We shall establish, maintain, and disseminate the national standards of units of measurements to provide international traceability to the measurements done in the country. We shall do this by competently conducting calibrations and measurements at accuracy levels appropriate to the needs of the customer. http://nml.gov.ph/about-nml/
Poland	Central Office of Measures www.gum.gov.pl/en	To ensure conformity and accuracy of the national measurement standards and their traceability to the international measurement standards. www.gum.gov.pl/en/about/main-tasks/99,Main-Tasks.html
Portugal	Portuguese Institute of Quality (IPQ) www1.ipq.pt/PT/Pages/Homepage.aspx	Ensuring the demand for the quality of products and services for the increase in the quality of life of citizens, increase in the competitiveness of economic activities in a context of progressive freedom of movement of goods. www1.ipq.pt/PT/IPQ/Pages/IPQ.aspx
Portugal	National Metrology Laboratory www1.ipq.pt/PT/Metrologia/Pages/Entrada0.aspx	To ensure the accuracy and traceability of measurements in the country through patterns and measurement required by industry and the Portuguese society and contribute to building a European metrology leadership. www1.ipq.pt/PT/Metrologia/Pages/Entrada0.aspx
Romania	National Institute of Metrology www.inm.ro/	To realize, maintain and disseminate units of measurement in Romania, in accordance with the requirements of the Mutual Recognition Arrangement of national measurement standards and Calibration and Measurement Certificates issued by the national institutes of metrology (CIPM-MRA). www.inm.ro/en/?page=mission

(*Continued*)

Table 3.1 (Continued) Description of national metrology laboratories, by country

Country (alphabetical)	*Laboratory*	*Mission statement / priority statement (quoted or translated)*
Russia (Republic of Belarus)	State Committee of the Russian Federation for Standardization, Metrology and Certification (GOSSTANDART) www.gosstandart.gov.by/en-US/	To ensure design and production of safe, high quality and competitive products and services, as well as to implement requirements of technical regulations adopted by the Customs Union. https://gosstandart.gov.by/en/general-information
Russia	All-Russian Scientific Research Institute for Physical and Radio-Technical Measurements (VNIIFTRI) www.vniiftri.ru/	Implements the reproduction of the national time scale and reference frequencies, determines the parameters of the Earth's rotation, develops, improves, maintains, compares, and applies the state primary standards of units, conducts fundamental and applied research, experimental development. www.vniiftri.ru/ru/about-us/o-vniiftri
Russia	All-Russian Research Institute for Optical and Physical Measurements (VNIIOFI) www.vniiofi.com/	Creating a state system for ensuring the uniformity of measurements in photometry, radiometry, optical radiation, parameters of pulsed electromagnetic fields. www.vniiofi.com/glavnaya/about-vniiofi.html
Russia	D.I. Mendeleyev Institute for Metrology (VNIIM) www.vniim.ru/	To ensure the uniformity of measurements in the country at the international level through the use of state standards of units of physical quantities, improvement of existing standards and the creation of new ones through fundamental and applied scientific research. www.vniim.ru/info.html
Russia	All-Russian Scientific Research Institute of Metrological Service (VNIIMS) www.vniims.ru/	[no specific mission statement]

Russia	Urals Scientific Research Institute of Metrology (UNIIM) www.uniim.ru/	[no specific mission statement]
Russia	West Siberian Branch of the FSUE (NIIFTRI) www.sniim.ru/	To form a position at the enterprise in which confidence in the measurement results is ensured, as well as continuous development of metrology, sufficient to provide effective metrological support for priority, promising tasks in vital areas of the economy, defense and social development, as in Russian Federation and the region. www.sniim.ru/index.php/2011-03-31-04-22-51
Russia	All-Russian Scientific Research Institute of Flowrate Measurement (VNIIR) www.vniir.ru/	[no specific mission statement]
Russia	"Dalnostandart" Scientific and Production Amalgamatic (NPO "Dalnostandart") [no website]	[no specific mission statement]
Russia	Eastern-Siberian Scientific Research Institute of Physico-Technical and Radiotechnical Measurements (VNIIFTRI) www.vniiftri.ru/en/vostochno-sibirskij-filial-eng	To provide enterprises, organizations, people with products and services in the field of metrology, conducts a set of research, development and engineering works for developing high-precision equipment for time and frequency and radio technical measurements, measurements of gas humidity, participates in the Federal target program for maintaining and improving the standard, scientific and technical base. www.vniiftri.ru/en/vostochno-sibirskij-filial-eng
Russia	Far Eastern Branch (VNIIFTRI) www.vniiftri.ru/en/dalnevostochnyj-eng	Ensuring the uniformity of measurements in the field of ultrasound measurements in solid media. www.vniiftri.ru/en/dalnevostochnyj-eng
Russia	Kahmkatsky Branch (VNIIFTRI)	[no specific mission statement]

(*Continued*)

Table 3.1 (Continued) Description of national metrology laboratories, by country

Country (alphabetical)	*Laboratory*	*Mission statement / priority statement (quoted or translated)*
Russia	All-Russian Scientific Research Centre of Standardization, Information and Certification of Raw Materials, Materials and Substances (VNICSMV)	[no specific mission statement]
Saudi Arabia	Saudi Arabian Standards Organization (SASO) www.saso.gov.sa/en/pages/default.aspx	Elevate the standards and the quality of products and services, to protect the consumer and to strengthen the competitiveness of the national economy. www.saso.gov.sa/en/about/Pages/vision.aspx
Seychelles	Seychelles Bureau of Standards www.sbs.sc/	To provide national and international capabilities to Seychelles in the areas of Standardization, Conformity Assessment (Inspection, Testing and Certification) and Metrology (Legal and Industrial). https://sbs.sc/mission-and-vision/
Singapore	A*Star www.a-star.edu.sg/nmc/	We advance science and develop innovative technology to further economic growth and improve lives. www.a-star.edu.sg/About-A-STAR/overview
Slovak Republic	Slovak Institute of Metrology www.unms.sk/?slovak-institute-of-metrology	Creation and development of the quality infrastructure tools. www.unms.sk/?the-mission-and-the-mid-term-perspective

Slovenia	Metrology Institute of the Republic of Slovenia www.mirs.gov.si/en/	The Metrology Institute establishes and manages the national metrology system. Thus, it ensures international comparability and recognizability while guaranteeing protection of consumers, especially in the areas of health protection, protection of the environment and general technical safety. In so doing, it helps the Slovenian economy to achieve international competitiveness. www.gov.si/en/state-authorities/bodies-within-ministries/metrology-institute/o-uradu-rs-za-meroslovje/
South Africa	National Metrology Laboratory, CSIR www.csir.co.za/	Collaboratively innovating and localizing technologies while providing knowledge solutions for the inclusive and sustainable advancement of industry and society. www.csir.co.za/about-us-0
South Africa	South African Bureau of Standards (SABS) www.sabs.co.za/	Provide standards and conformity assessment services to enable the efficient functioning of the economy. www.sabs.co.za/About-SABS/about_vision.asp
Spain	Centro Español de Metrologia www.cem.es/	Custody, conservation and dissemination of national standards of measurement units; traceability support to the network of calibration and testing laboratories and industry; exercise of the functions of the General State Administration in matters of legal metrology; execution of research and development projects in the metrological field; management of the Metrological Control Registry; training of specialists in metrology; representation of Spain before international metrological organizations. www.cem.es/cem
St. Kitts and Nevis	St. Kitts and Nevis Bureau of Standards www.sknbs.org/	To deliver the highest quality of service in the areas of metrology, food, water and environmental testing and monitor compliance to related standards and regulations in order to foster the improved quality of life for the people of St. Kitts and Nevis. www.sknbs.org/who-we-are/
St. Lucia	Saint Lucia Bureau of Standards www.slbs.org/	To strengthen the national quality infrastructure in Saint Lucia in order to contribute to the advancement of the national economy, support sustainable development, promote health and safety of consumers, protect the environment, and facilitate trade. www.slbs.org/about-us/

(*Continued*)

Table 3.1 (Continued) Description of national metrology laboratories, by country

Country (alphabetical)	*Laboratory*	*Mission statement / priority statement (quoted or translated)*
St. Vincent and Grenadines	St. Vincent and Grenadines Bureau of Standards www.linkedin.com/company/st-vincent-and-the-grenadines-bureau-of-standards/	To prepare and promote standards relating to goods, services, processes and practices produced and/or used in St. Vincent and the Grenadines, to ensure industrial efficiency and to assist in industrial development as well as to promote public and industrial welfare, health, safety and to safeguard against negative effects to the environment. www.linkedin.com/company/st-vincent-and-the-grenadines-bureau-of-standards/about/
Suriname	Suriname Standards Bureau (SSB) http://tradeandindustry.gov.sr/diensten/surinaams-standaarden-bureau-ssb/	To create an adequate, healthy standard infrastructure to stimulate economic activities, to protect the environment, human safety and health, and to protect the life and health of plants and animals, by means of establishing, adopting, developing, maintaining and promoting the application and use of standards and technical regulations. http://tradeandindustry.gov.sr/diensten/surinaams-standaarden-bureau-ssb/
Sweden	Swedish National Testing and Research Institute www.sp.se/en/Sidor/default.aspx	Accelerating innovation. www.ri.se/sv/om-rise/vision-och-mission
Switzerland	Federal Office of Metrology (METAS) www.metas.ch/metas/en/home.html	To ensure the availability in Switzerland of measurement and testing facilities with the degree of accuracy needed to meet the requirements of the economy, research, and administration. www.metas.ch/metas/en/home/metas/institut.html
Taiwan	Industrial Technology Research Institute www.itri.org.tw/eng/	To drive industrial development, create economic value, and enhance social well-being through technology R&D. www.itri.org.tw/english/ListStyle.aspx?DisplayStyle=20&SiteID=1&MmmID=617731521661672477
Tanzania	Tanzania Bureau of Standards http://tbs.go.tz/	To promote standardization and quality assurance in industry and commerce through standards development, certification, inspection, testing and metrology services for sustainable socio-economic development. www.tbs.go.tz/index.php/tbs/aboutus/category/mission_and_vision

Thailand	National Institute of Metrology (Thailand) www.nimt.or.th/main/	Procure, develop and maintain national measurement standards and reference material which is accepted internationally to meet the needs of domestic users; create a network and develop analytical laboratories testing and calibration in the country to have enough to meet the needs and is accepted internationally; integration in creation and develop quality infrastructure to be accepted internationally; develop knowledge in metrology in order to create innovation, enhance manufacturing; and service sector capabilities. including other economic sectors within the country; and make an impact on the quality of life of people such as trade and consumer protection, public health, and environmental safety. www.nimt.or.th/main/?page_id=8049
Trinidad and Tobago	Trinidad and Tobago Bureau of Standards https://gottbs.com/	To champion the development and implementation of standards, measurement systems and conformity assessment services for the competitiveness and sustainability of Trinidad and Tobago. https://gottbs.com/mandate-mission-vision/#.Xtf9UDpKhPY
Tunisia	Institut nacional de la Normalisation et de la Propriété Industrielle www.innorpi.tn/	Centralize and coordinate all work, studies, and surveys in these various fields Decides, in collaboration with the organizations concerned, the general program for developing standards, creates technical standardization committees. Organizes their work within it and provides the secretariat. INNORPI is the national information point on standards. Certifies compliance with standards for products, services and management systems and manages national brands of compliance with standards. Issuing invention patents, registering trademarks, service, and industrial designs. Receives and records all acts affecting industrial property rights. Represent Tunisia to the International Organization for Standardization ISO, the International Electrotechnical Commission IEC, the World Intellectual Property Organization, WIPO, the Arab Organization for Industrial Development and Mining AIDMO, the African Organization for Standardization ARSO and the European Patent Office EPO. www.innorpi.tn/fr/propos-de-linnorpi

(*Continued*)

Table 3.1 (Continued) Description of national metrology laboratories, by country

Country (alphabetical)	*Laboratory*	*Mission statement / priority statement (quoted or translated)*
Turkey	Tübitak Ulusal Metroloji Enstitüsü (UME) www.ume.tubitak.gov.tr/en	To conduct research and development in the area of metrology towards the establishment and of uniformity and reliability in measurements through the development, improvement, maintenance and dissemination of internationally accepted reference measurement standards and techniques for the purpose of contributing to the nation's quality of life and economic competitiveness. www.ume.tubitak.gov.tr/en/kurumsal/who-we-are
Uganda	Ministry of Trade, Industry, and Cooperatives www.mtic.go.ug/	To enhance national development through the application of standards in trade, industry to encourage fair competition and protect consumers. www.mtic.go.ug/uganda-national-bureau-of-standards/
Uganda	Uganda National Bureau of Standards www.unbs.go.ug/	To provide standards, measurements, and conformity assessment services for improved quality of life. www.unbs.go.ug//content.php?src=mission-and-vision&pg=content
Ukraine	SE "Ukrmetrteststandard" https://ukrcsm.kiev.ua/index.php/en/	Product certification in the state certification system; assessment of product compliance with the requirements of 20 Technical Regulations; certification of 5 management systems. https://ukrcsm.kiev.ua/index.php/en/home-ua/powers-ua
Ukraine	National Scientific Center "Institute of Metrology" www.metrology.kharkov.ua/index.php?id=1&L=2	Conducts basic and applied scientific research in the field of metrology and performs research work related to the creation, enhancement, storage, use of primary and secondary standards, the creation of transmission systems of units of measurement, development of normative documents Metrology, the formation of the state programs in metrology and the concept of development of the state metrological system and performs the state metrological control and scientific and methodological support of metrology in Ukraine. www.metrology.kharkov.ua/index.php?id=nsc_im_abouthtml&L=2

United Kingdom	National Physical Laboratory (NPL) www.npl.co.uk/	To provide the measurement capability that underpins the UK's prosperity and quality of life. www.npl.co.uk/about-us/national-metrology-institute
United States	National Institute of Standards and Technology www.nist.gov/	To promote U.S. innovation and industrial competitiveness by advancing measurement science, standards, and technology in ways that enhance economic security and improve our quality of life. www.nist.gov/about-nist/our-organization/mission-vision-values
Uruguay	Laboratorio Tecnológico del Uruguay www.latu.org.uy/	To promote the sustainable development of the country and its international insertion through innovation and transfer of value solutions in the field of tests and assays, conformity assessment, metrology, technology, the promotion of a scientific and entrepreneurial culture and the development of technological platforms. www.latu.org.uy/en/institutional/about
Venezuela	Servicio Autónomo Nacional de Metrología (SENCAMER) www.sencamer.gob.ve/	Guarantee the quality of goods and services acquired by Venezuelans, through the normalization, metrology, accreditation, certifications, technical regulations and testing subsystems, based on socialist principles of the Bolivarian revolution www.sencamer.gob.ve/?q=content/misi%C3%B3n-y-visi%C3%B3n
Vietnam	Directorate for Standards, Metrology, and Quality (STAMEQ) https://tcvn.gov.vn/?lang=en	To advise the Government on issues in the fields of standardization, metrology, productivity, and quality management in the country and representing Vietnam in relevant international and regional organizations. https://tcvn.gov.vn/general-information/?lang=en
Zambia	Zambia Bureau of Standards (ZABS) www.zabs.org.zm/	To efficiently and effectively provide standardization and quality assurance services in order to promote competitiveness of industry and quality culture so as to contribute to sustainable socio-economic development. www.zabs.org.zm/who-we-are/overview/who-we-are.html

(*Continued*)

Table 3.1 (Continued) Description of national metrology laboratories, by country

Country (alphabetical)	*Laboratory*	*Mission statement / priority statement (quoted or translated)*
Zambia	Zambia Compulsory Standards Agency (ZCSA) www.zcsa.org.zm/index.php	To administer, maintain and ensure compliance with compulsory standards for the purpose of public safety and health, consumer protection and environmental protection. www.zcsa.org.zm/index.php/who-we-are/about-zcsa
Zambia	Zambia Metrology Agency (ZMA) www.zma.org.zm/	To provide metrology services to industry, research institutions and the public in order to promote the quality and competitiveness of products and services and guarantee fair trade and consumer protection. www.zma.org.zm/mandate-vision-mission.php
Zimbabwe	Scientific and Industrial Research and Development Centre www.sirdc.ac.zw/	To provide Zimbabwe and the region with technological solutions for sustainable development. www.sirdc.ac.zw/about/vision/

Notes: I am indebted to Kelsi Hobbs for her excellent research assistance on the preparation of this table.
All websites accessed and verified on December 8, 2020.

Notes

1 Some measurement standards are pure public goods, such as material characteristics and associated measurement methods. Other measurement standards are quasi-public goods, having been promulgated by industry, such as test methods and calibration procedures for equipment and process control. See Tassey (2017).

2 Swann's original statement did not use the phrase *measurement infrastructures*; Swann used the term *infratechnologies*, a term traceable to Tassey (1982). Swann's (2009, p. v) use of the term *infratechnologies* was intended to refer to "the technologies that provide the infrastructure for further innovation." According to Tassey (1982, p. 163): "infratechnologies are necessary for the evolution of the generic technology and its applications." See also Tassey (2010).

3 See www.nist.gov/about-nist/our-organization/mission-vision-values (accessed December 30, 2020).

4 This section draws directly from earlier writings about the history of measurement standards and of NIST; see Link and Scott (1998), Link (2019), and especially Link (2021). And, the material in these references draws directly from Cochrane (1966). See also Frazier (1978) and Martin and Silcox (2010). This historical trace is offered for the purpose of context, and it is not intended to cause the reader to divagate from the theme of this chapter.

5 See Spencer and Temple (2016) for the early history of the British Standards Institution.

6 Perhaps it was fitting that this meeting was held in France because the origins of the metric system can be traced to the research of Gabriel Mouton, a French vicar, in the late 1600s. His standard unit was based on the length of an arc of one minute of a great circle of the earth. Given controversy, the National Assembly of France decreed on May 8, 1790, that the French Academy of Sciences along with the Royal Society of London deduce an invariable standard for all the measures and all the weights.

7 See De Simone and Treat (1971) for an history of the metric system in the United States.

8 There were a number of Congressional responses to this productivity slowdown, but the scope of motivation for several legislative initiatives was broader than the productivity slowdown. For example, as stated in the Joint Research and Development Act of 1984: "Joint research and development as our foreign competitors have learned [Japan] can be pro-competitive. It can reduce duplication, promote the efficient use of scarce technical personnel, and help to achieve desirable economies of scale [in R&D]."

9 The section (Subtitle B, Part I) of the Omnibus Trade and Competitiveness Act from which this excerpt about the National Bureau of Standards and the National Institute of Standards and Technology is quoted is called the Technology Competitiveness Act.

10 Seiler (1999) discusses a number of these agencies.

4 Measurement standards activities at the National Institute of Standards and Technology

Quantifying NIST's measurement standards activities

The Technology Partnerships Office at NIST publishes metrics associated with four mechanisms related to its activities to support existing or developing measurement standards.[1] These metrics are related to various measurement standards activities ranging from staff participation in standards processes to calibration testing services for firms and organizations. As a group, these measurement standards activities represent mechanisms through which the outputs of NIST based measurement science research are transferred to society. These measurement standards activities represent the embodiment of scientific knowledge—mostly codified scientific knowledge—being transferred to society. While not traditionally viewed as technology transfer mechanisms—a so-called mirepoix of technology transfer mechanisms has traditionally included patents, licences, and CRADAs (cooperative research and development agreements)—these measurement standards activities possibly should be so viewed (Leyden and Link, 2015; Link and Oliver, 2000).[2]

As background, and to provide context, Figure 4.1 shows the fiscal year (FY) research budgets at NIST over the fiscal years of FY 1990 through FY 2020.[3] As shown, the research laboratory budgets at NIST have increased steadily over time, and they have been less sporadic than the budgets of NIST as an agency. Also, the percentage of NIST's budgets allocated to the research laboratories has been increasing over the past two decades relative to the agency's overall budgets (i.e., the vertical gap between the trend lines in the figure has been decreasing).

Available data related to the first transfer mechanism considered herein to support existing or developed measurement standards relate to the number of NIST staff who have participated in documentary standards. According to NIST:[4]

DOI: 10.4324/9781003186953-4

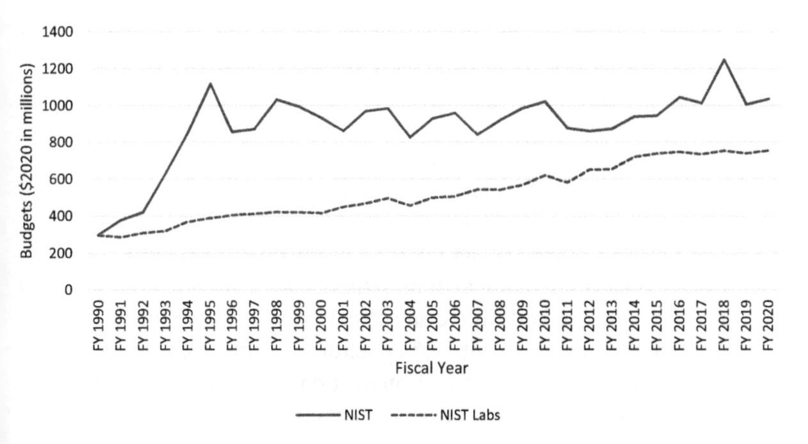

Figure 4.1 Budgets for NIST and for NIST's research laboratories, FY 1990–FY 2020 ($2020 in millions). Source: www.aaas.org/programs/r-d-budget-and-policy/historical-trends-federal-rd (accessed December 4, 2020).

> Documentary Standards can specify definition of terms; classifications of components; delineation of procedures; specification of dimensions, materials, processes, products, systems, services or practices; test methods and sampling procedures; or descriptions of fit and measurements of size or strength. Under the National Technology Transfer and Advancement Act (NTTAA) [of 1995, Public Law 104-113], NIST is assigned responsibility to coordinate federal, state, and local documentary standards and conformity assessment activities.

Leech and Scott (2011, p. 26), for example, recently conducted under the sponsorship of NIST an economic impact evaluation of one documentary standard, the Flat Panel Display Measurement Standard which relates to "the characterization, specification, qualification, and assessment of flat panel displays for a broad range of uses that could not be adequately addressed by a range of existing related standards." These authors offered in their final report to NIST a more complete description of a documentary standard (2011, p. 26):

> Documentary standards are written agreements among producers and/or users of products and services containing technical specifications or other precise criteria that may contain rules, guidelines, or definitions of characteristics. These standards ensure that materials, products,

personnel qualifications, processes, and services are adequate for their purpose, compatible and/or interchangeable, if necessary; ensure public health and safety; protect the environment; and/or improve economic performance.

Documentary standards can specify product characteristics, establish accepted test methods and procedures, characterize materials, define processes and systems, or specify knowledge, training and competencies for specific tasks.

Frequently (perhaps optimally), documentary standards act as a bridge connecting national representations of international physical measurement standards to the day-to day operations of industry in their research and development (R&D) efforts; in the application of this R&D to new technologies and innovations; and in transitioning new products and services into growing markets.

Figure 4.2 shows the number of NIST staff who participated with standards organizations in the process of developing documentary standards over the fiscal years of FY 2013 through FY 2019.

Available data on the second transfer mechanism relate to the number of downloads of standard reference data (SRD) from NIST websites over the fiscal years of FY 2011 through FY 2019. See Figure 4.3. The Standard Reference Data Act of 1968 (Public Law 90-396) was passed by Congress in that year. The act authorized and directed the Secretary of the Department of Commerce to provide or arrange for the collection,

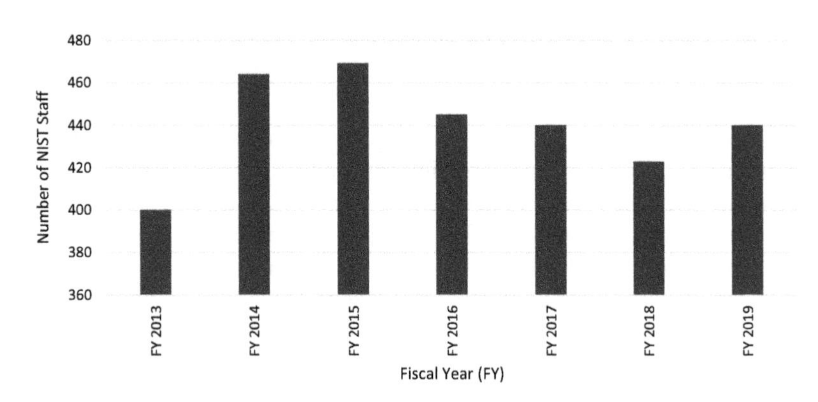

Figure 4.2 Number of NIST staff who participated with standards organizations in the process of developing documentary standards, by fiscal year. Source: www.nist.gov/tpo/department-commerce (accessed December 13, 2020).

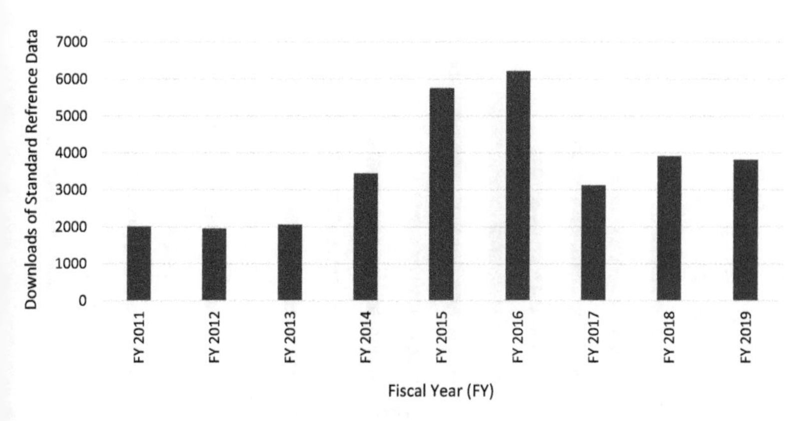

Figure 4.3 Downloads of standard reference data (SRD) from the NIST website, by fiscal year. Source: www.nist.gov/tpo/department-commerce (accessed December 13, 2020).

compilation, critical evaluation, publication, and dissemination of standard reference data. In 2017, Congress passed the Standard Reference Data Act Update (Public Law 114-329), with an expanded definition of SRD to include either:[5]

(1) quantitative information related to a measurable physical, or chemical, or biological property of a substance or system of substances of known composition and structure;
(2) measurable characteristics of a physical artifact or artifacts;
(3) engineering properties or performance characteristics of a system; or
(4) one or more digital data objects that serve –
to calibrate or characterize the performance of a detection or measurement system;
or to interpolate or extrapolate, or both, data described in (1)–(3);
and that is critically evaluated as to its reliability under section 290b of this title.

Available data on the third transfer mechanism relate to the number of units of standard reference materials (SRMs) sold by NIST over the fiscal years of FY 1999 through FY 2018. See Figure 4.4. *Reference material* is a generic term that refers to material that is sufficiently homogeneous and stable with respect to one or more specified properties and which is already

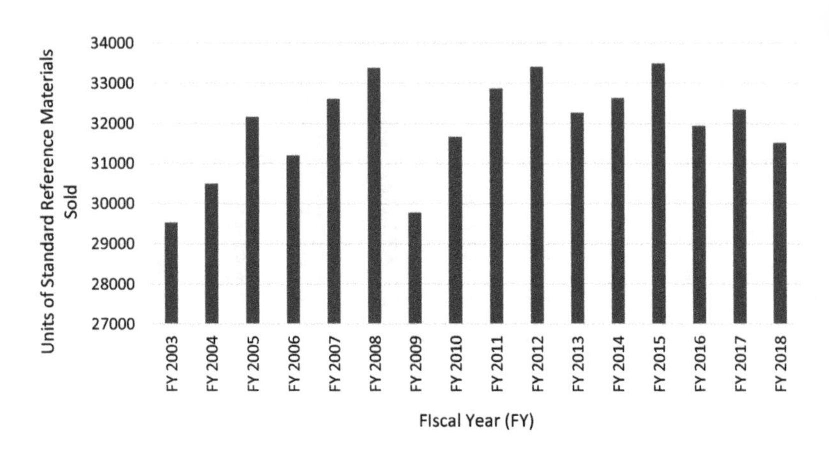

Figure 4.4 Units of standard reference materials (SRMs) sold by NIST by fiscal year. Source: www.nist.gov/tpo/department-commerce (accessed December 14, 2020). Note: The decrease in SRMs sold in FY 2009 might reflect market purchasing aspects associated with the Great Recession.

established to be fit for its intended use in a measurement process. Standard reference material, according to NIST:[6]

> is prepared and used for three main purposes: (1) to help develop accurate methods of analysis; (2) to calibrate measurement systems used to facilitate exchange of goods, institute quality control, determine performance characteristics, or measure a property at the state-of-the-art limit; and (3) to ensure the long-term adequacy and integrity of measurement quality assurance programs. The term "Standard Reference Material" is registered with the United States Patent and Trademark Office.

Available data on the fourth transfer mechanism relate to calibration testing services. Figure 4.5 shows the number of calibration tests performed at NIST over the fiscal years of FY 1999 through FY 2018. According to NIST (USDOC, 2019, p. 24):[7]

> The NIST laboratories provide unique physical measurement services for their customers, including calibration services, special tests, and measurement assurance programs. NIST designs its calibration services to help manufacturers and users of precision instruments achieve the highest possible levels of measurement quality and productivity [i.e., to achieve accuracy and consistency of performance]. NIST calibrations often serve as the basis for companies that provide commercial calibration services and calibration equipment.

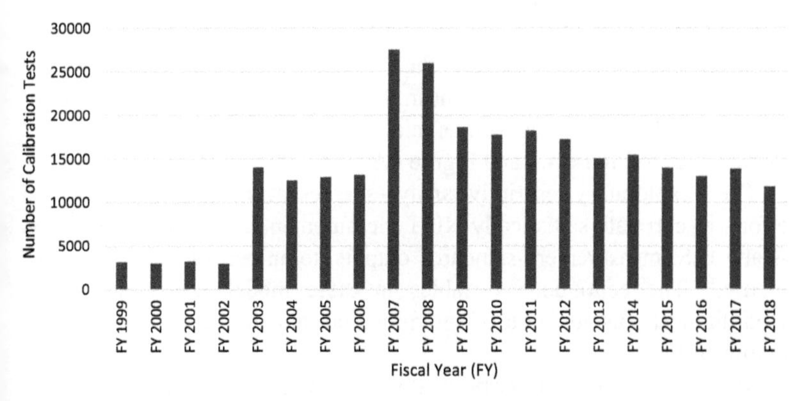

Figure 4.5 Calibration tests performed at NIST, by fiscal year. Source: www.nist.gov/tpo/department-commerce (accessed December 14, 2020). Note: In the source for these data, NIST noted that in FY 2003, it "accredited 72 calibration laboratories in fields ranging from dimensional metrology to optical and chemical. Through this overall approach, NIST efficiently leverages its primary calibration services to support a broader base of secondary calibrations conducted within the private sector." This accounts for the increase in calibration tests from 2002 to 2003. Also, in the source for these data, NIST noted that the "number of calibration tests performed in 2007 was significantly higher than the number of tests performed in FY 2005 and FY 2006 due principally to a surge in the calibration testing for the military and its contractors." Also, the number of calibration tests shown in this figure by fiscal year are greater than the number that will be considered in Chapter 5. The reason for this is because of the NIST National Voluntary Laboratory Accreditation Program (NVLAP). This is a voluntary and fee-supported program to accredit private sector laboratories that are found competent to perform specific tests or calibrations, or types of tests or calibrations. Through NVLAP, NIST efficiently leverages its primary calibration services to support a broader base of secondary calibrations conducted within the private sector.

Economic impacts associated with NIST's measurement standards activities

There are a sufficient number of annual data on units of standard reference materials and number of calibration tests that are shown in Figure 4.4 and Figure 4.5, respectively, to allow for an exploratory descriptive study of the relationship between data on each of these two measurement standards transfer mechanisms and a measure of aggregate economic performance. In an effort to contribute to the extant literature that is based on specification similar to that presented in equation (2.1),[8] an exploratory descriptive analysis of the relationship between aggregate industrial multifactor productivity (*MFP*)[9] and the number of units of standard reference materials (*SRM*) sold by NIST and separately the number of calibration tests (*Calibrate*) conducted at NIST in the FYs shown in Figure 4.4 and Figure 4.5 was considered. Held constant in these separate models is the level of national R&D (*R&D*)[10] as well as related fixed effects (*Dmy*) as described in the Notes to Figure 4.4 and Figure 4.5.

These exploratory descriptive analyses represent one of the first empirical efforts to correlate statistically NIST measurement standards outputs, that is any U.S. measurement standards outputs, to an economic performance metric.[11] The continuous variables in these models are measured in logarithmic terms for ease of interpretation and to account for possible nonlinearities.[12]

Table 4.1 presents descriptive statistics on the relevant variables for these exploratory descriptive analyses using the following regression model specifications that mirror models that have previously been used in the literature:[13]

$$\log MFP = \alpha_1 + \beta_1 \log SRM + \gamma_1 \log R\&D + Dmy + \varepsilon \tag{4.1}$$

$$\log MFP = \alpha_2 + \beta_2 \log Calibrate + \gamma_2 \log R\&D + Dmy + \varepsilon \tag{4.2}$$

Table 4.1 Descriptive statistics on the variables in equation (4.1) and the regression results

Variable	*Mean*	*Standard deviation*	*Range*
MFP	96.9426	4.5747	87.7190–102.7940
SRM	32080.15	1235.45	29527–34020
Calibrate	13631.70	6796.26	2924–27489
R&D	413858.90	59229.37	320086–525256

Regression results from equations (4.1) and (4.2)
log *MFP* dependent variable

Regressor	*(1) Coefficient (standard error)*	*(2) Coefficient (standard error)*
log *SRM*	0.1492** (0.0403)	–
log *Calibrate*	–	0.0170*** (0.0048)
log *R&D*	0.1905*** (0.0285)	0.2136*** (0.0236)
R-squared	0.9330	0.9571
Durbin-Watson	2.091	2.158
n	16	20

Note: Earlier preliminary versions of the results in column (2) were reported in Link (2021).
*** significant at .01-level, ** significant at .05-level

where the error term, ε, in both equations is assumed to obey all of the classical assumptions.

Based on findings reported in the literature for other countries, the estimated values of β_1 and β_2 and of γ_1 and γ_2 are expected to be positive.[14] The regression results from the estimation of these models are also presented in Table 4.1. The results from equation (4.1) are in column (1) of the lower part of the table, and the results from equation (4.2) are in column (2) of the lower part of the table.

The estimated coefficient on log *SRM* in column (1) is positive and statistically significant. It suggests that a 10 percent increase in the number of units of standard reference materials sold is associated with a 1.5 percent increase in the multifactor productivity index. The estimated coefficient on log *Calibrate* is positive and statistically significant. It suggests that a 10 percent increase in the number of calibration tests is associated with a 0.17 percent increase in the multifactor productivity index. The numerical size of this elasticity measure is not the point.[15] The point to suggest is that U.S. measurement standards are positively related to measured productivity growth in the country.

In Chapter 5, additional data related to calibration tests at NIST are considered.

Notes

1 See USDOC (2019) and previous years of the annual report from the Technology Partnerships Office. These mechanisms are discussed below. The order in which I discuss these mechanisms should not be interpreted to reflect either the NIST importance of the mechanisms or the social importance of the mechanisms.
2 Link (2019) makes references to these measurement standards activities in the context of technology transfer, but they are not included in the analysis therein.
3 I thank Greg Tassey for reminding me that not all of NIST's research laboratory budget in a given fiscal year represents investments in measurement science. For example, NIST also maintains a growing computer security program. Standards are developed in the research laboratories at NIST to implement and manage security systems, but the systems themselves rely on the laboratory's budget.
4 See www.nist.gov/topics/documentary-standards (accessed December 30, 2020).
5 See www.nist.gov/srd/srd-definition (accessed December 30, 2020).
6 See www.nist.gov/srm/srm-definitions (accessed December 30, 2020).
7 In chemistry, "Calibration is the process of relating a known quantity of an analyte to the corresponding measured instrumental response through a mathematical relationship. Calibration permits the assignment of analyte levels in unknown samples based on the known levels of the calibrants." See www.nist .gov/video/calibration (accessed November 30, 2020).

8 In particular, see the studies by Temple and Williams (2002) who considered changes in total factor productivity in the United Kingdom, and Choudhary et al. (2013) who considered bilateral trade among European Union countries.
9 These calendar year data come from the Bureau of Labor Statistics (www.bls.gov/mfp/tables.htm), accessed October 22, 2020, and they refer to the U.S. private business sector (2012=100).
10 These calendar year data, in $2012 in millions, come from the National Science Foundation. See https://ncses.nsf.gov/pubs/nsf20307/#& (accessed November 12, 2020). See also Hall et al. (2010).
11 This analysis parallels in concept the aggregate studies of measurement standards discussed in relation to equation (2.1) above. In an effort to address the criticism as mentioned regarding the use of an estimating model like equation (2.1) that does not control for investments in R&D, the log of NIST's laboratory R&D budget (see Figure 4.1) was also considered as a regressor. The estimated coefficient was positive, but it was not statistically significant at a conventional level.
12 Link (2021) considered a more complete two-stage specification of the relationship between calibration tests and multifactor productivity than that in equation (4.2). The parsimonious specification is presented here to parallel the analysis on standard reference materials; the data on SRMs is more limited over time than the data on calibration tests.
13 For comparison, see equation (2.1).
14 No relationship between the values of β_1 and β_2 or between the values of γ_1 and γ_2 is hypothesized.
15 An important point should be emphasized about the size of the estimated calibration elasticity, β_2, from equation (4.2). The internal use of NIST's calibration standards, that is the internal organizational calibrations traceable to the NIST primary standard, has a much larger impact on economic activity than does the number of calibration tests conducted at NIST.

5 Calibration testing at the National Institute of Standards and Technology

Description of the data

As referenced in Chapter 4 with respect to calibration tests:

> The NIST laboratories provide unique physical measurement services for their customers, including calibration services, special tests, and measurement assurance programs. NIST designs its calibration services to help manufacturers and users of precision instruments achieve the highest possible levels of measurement quality and productivity. NIST calibrations often serve as the basis for companies that provide commercial calibration services and calibration equipment.

The data used in this section of the book relate to the 1,838 organizational customers that requested over the fiscal years of FY 2010 through FY 2014 a for-fee calibration test to be performed at NIST.[1] The customers for calibration tests are global, but only those customers in the "lower 48" of the United States are considered in the exploratory spatial analysis that follows.[2] These data are studied for the purpose of developing and presenting stylized facts about calibration testing at NIST.

Regarding the sectors corresponding to the 1,838 calibration customers from NIST, 73.5 percent of the customers were U.S. corporations, 23.9 percent were federal agencies including federal laboratories, and 2.6 percent were state and local organizations including universities. See Figure 5.1.

To illustrate that the entire United States benefits from the availability of NIST calibration testing in a manner that complements the implications from the regression analysis presented in Chapter 4, the percentage of the 1,838 calibration customers within various mileage categories from Gaithersburg, MD, where NIST's main campus is located, was calculated.[3] See Table 5.1. Of course, the distribution of potential customers for calibration tests is not distributed evenly across the country because the population

DOI: 10.4324/9781003186953-5

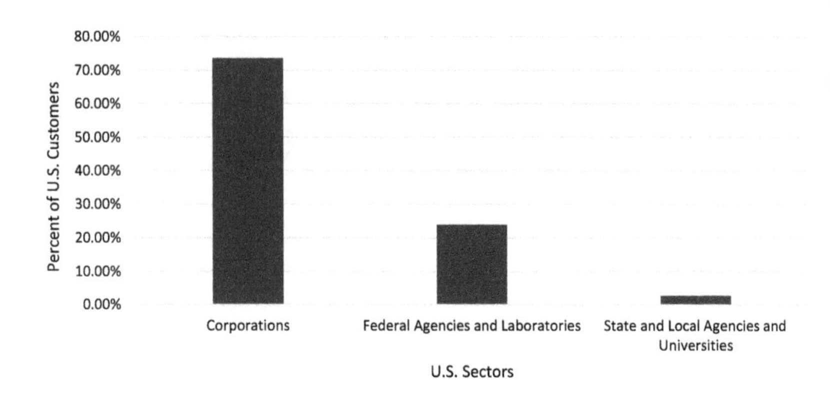

Figure 5.1 Distribution of calibration test customers, by sector (n=1,838)

Table 5.1 Geographic distribution of calibration test customers from NIST, FY 2009 through FY 2014 (n=1,838)

Distance of calibration test customers from NIST in Gaithersburg, MD	*Percent of all calibration tests*	*Percent of all calibration tests less those performed for NIST (Gaithersburg) scientists*
100 miles or less	10.99%	4.88%
101–250 miles	7.34%	7.85%
251–500 miles	18.93%	20.23%
501–750 miles	16.92%	18.08%
751–1,000 miles	5.17%	5.52%
1,001–1,250 miles	2.07%	2.21%
1,251–1,500 miles	9.14%	9.77%
1,501–1,750 miles	4.03%	4.30%
1,751–2,000 miles	3.05%	3.26%
2,001–2,225 miles	1.74%	1.86%
2,226–2,500 miles	2.39%	2.56%
More than 2,500 miles	18.28%	19.53%
	100% (rounded)	100% (rounded)

Notes: NIST has a smaller campus in Boulder, CO.

of potential customers is not distributed evenly across the country, but the distribution is countrywide as might be expected because calibrations represent applied codified knowledge for the user rather than applied tacit knowledge that needed to be acquired in a face-to-face manner through interactions with scientists at NIST. More than one half of the calibration tests at NIST over the five-fiscal-year periods for which data were made available were conducted for corporations or corporate division customers located east of the Mississippi River (54.18%). Moving west from the Mississippi River, the largest cluster of calibration test customers is along the west coast (California, Oregon, and Washington)—18.28%.

Over this five-fiscal-year period, 118 calibration tests were conducted at NIST laboratories for use by the NIST laboratories. If those calibrations tests, which are obviously within 100 miles of NIST, are deleted from the above calculations, the distance distribution of calibration tests is similar as shown in the last column of Table 5.1.

A calibration test customer might have requested, in a given fiscal year, more than one calibration test to be performed. For example, the 1,838 customers requested a total of 5,531 separate calibration tests over the five-fiscal-year period to which the NIST data relate. Figure 5.2 shows that corporations and their corporate divisions accounted for 57.7 percent of the calibration tests, 41.1 percent were requested by federal agencies and laboratories, and 1.2 percent were requested by state and local agencies and universities.

The remaining empirical focus of this chapter is on corporate calibration tests. Table 5.2 shows the distribution of corporate calibration tests by the number of requested tests. Nearly 85 percent of the corporations and corporate divisions requested only one calibration test over the five fiscal years of data.

As noted above, the National Bureau of Economic Research (NBER) has dated the Great Recession to have occurred in the United States from December 2007 through June 2009. The NIST data on calibration tests for FY 2010 begins on October 1, 2009, so the NIST data do not capture calibrations that were requested during the Great Recession. Figure 5.3 shows the distribution of calibration tests requested by corporations over the five-fiscal-year period. Nearly 36 percent of all calibration tests were begun in FY 2010, and the percentages are less in each of the following fiscal years. Perhaps FY 2010 represents a rebounding year after the Great Recession.

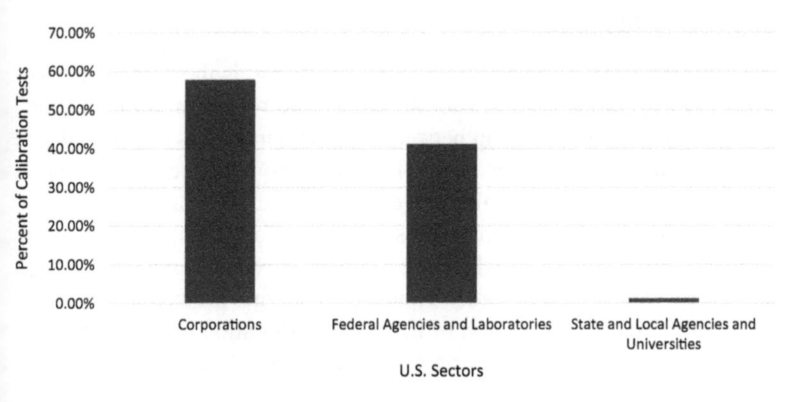

Figure 5.2 Distribution of calibration tests, by sector (n=5,531)

Table 5.2 Distribution of calibration tests by corporations and corporate divisions, FY 2010 through FY 2014 (n=3,191)

Number of calibration tests	*Percent of all calibration tests*
1	84.72%
2–5	9.59%
6–10	2.77%
11–15	1.12%
16–20	0.45%
21–25	0.15%
26–30	0.30%
31–35	0.22%
36 and greater	0.67%
	100% (rounded)

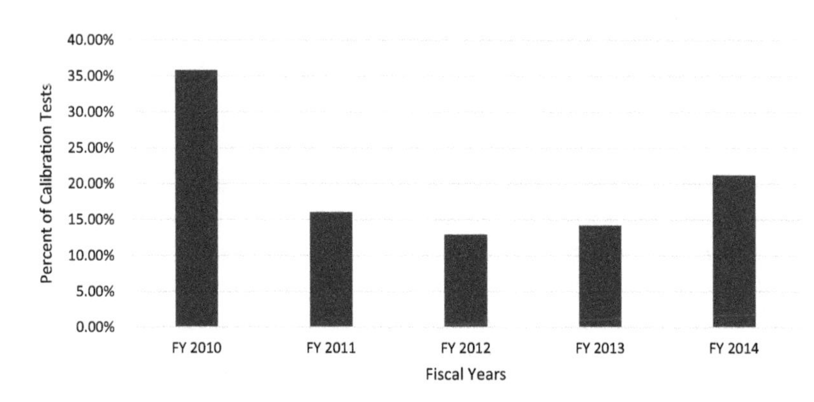

Figure 5.3 Distribution of calibration tests requested by corporations, by fiscal year (n=3,191)

Analysis of the data

The question asked in this section is the following: is the number of calibration tests requested related to the size of the requesting organization? The hypothesized relationship between the number of tests (*Tests*) and size as measured by the number of employees (*Emp*) is expected to be positive based on the argument that larger entities (i.e., corporation or corporate divisions) have greater resources for calibration testing[4] and are more diverse in the activities to which the calibration results apply. Thus, such entities can utilize the calibration results over a larger production scale.

To quantify the size of each of the 1,838 corporation or corporate divisions that requested a calibration test over the five fiscal years, an effort

was made to match each customer with information in the National Establishment Time-Series (NETS) Database.[5] When available, the number of employees was collected as a measure of size, and the primary industry in which each corporation or corporate division operated was collected at the 2-digit NAICS level. Both data series were collected for the year 2012, the year that is the median fiscal year of the five fiscal years of calibration test data. For this matching, the complete address of the corporation or corporate division in the NIST dataset had to match *exactly* [emphasis added] with the address of an enterprise in the NETS database. This occurred only 310 times. The primary reason for the fewness of matches was because many of the corporations in the NIST calibration dataset are private and are very small. Thus, they are rarely captured, if at all, in the NETS database. The sample of 310 corporations or corporate divisions is not presented herein as representative of the population of corporations or corporate divisions that requested calibration tests at NIST. The data in this sample should be viewed only as descriptive information that is part of this exploratory study. Table 5.3 shows descriptive statistics on this sample.
To test empirically this hypothesis, the following regression model was considered:

$$\log Tests = \alpha + \beta \log Emp + \gamma Ind33 + \eta Ind54 + \varepsilon \tag{5.1}$$

where the error term, ε, is assumed to obey all classical assumptions. The regression results from this model are presented in Table 5.4. Also held constant in equation (5.1) are selected industry fixed effects. Based on Table 5.3, the largest (in terms of the number of users of calibration tests) two two-digit NAICS industries represented in the sample of 310 firms or organizations is NAICS 33 (*Ind33*) and NAICS 54 (*Ind54*).[6]

The estimated coefficient on log (*Emp*) is positive, as hypothesized, and statistically significant. A 10 percent increase in employment is associated with a 1.46 percent increase in calibration tests. The estimated coefficient on *Ind33*, the binary variable that controls for whether the corporation or the corporate division is primarily reported in the NAICS industry 33 (Primary and Fabricated Metal Manufacturing, Computer and Electronics Manufacturing) is negative and statistically significant.

Summary remarks of the previous chapters are offered in Chapter 6. In addition, suggestions for a roadmap for future research on the economics of metrology are offered. Clearly, more research is needed on the characteristics of organizations that utilize NIST's calibration testing services.

Table 5.3 Descriptive statistics on private sector enterprises and divisions variables (n=310)

NAICS	*Number of Corporations and Corporate Divisions*	*Mean Number Calibration Tests*	*Mean Number of Employees*
21	2	1.5	51.0
22	11	5.3	3557.3
23	1	1	13.0
31	1	1	6.0
32	17	3.6	3383.5
33	153	3.1	1242.1
42	26	2	107.3
44	2	3	19.5
48	4	2	175.5
51	3	2.7	1813
52	2	2	19.5
53	1	1	470.0
54	64	2.6	417.6
56	5	6.8	350.8
61	1	1	12.0
62	4	5	155.3
81	13	2.8	36.0

Key to NAICS industries
21: Mining, Quarrying, and Oil and Gas Extraction
22: Utilities
23: Construction
31: Food Manufacturing
32: Paper Manufacturing, Chemical Manufacturing, Non-metallic Mineral Manufacturing
33: Primary and Fabricated Metal Manufacturing, Computer and Electronics Manufacturing
42: Wholesale Trade
44: Motor Vehicles and Parts Dealers
48: Air and Truck Transportation
51: Information
52: Finance and Insurance
53: Real Estate and Rental and Leasing
54: Professional, Scientific, and Technical Services
56: Administrative and Support and Waste Management and Remediation Services
61: Educational Services
62: Health Care and Social Assistance
81: Other Services (except Public Administration)

Table 5.4 Regression results from equation (5.1), log *Tests* is the dependent variable (n=310)

Regressor	*Coefficient (standard error)*
Intercept	0.1097
	(0.112)
log *Emp*	0.1460***
	(0.019)
Ind33	−0.1663*
	(0.100)
Ind54	0.1000
	(0.124)
R-squared	0.172
F-statistic	21.06***

*** significant at .01 level, * significant at .10 level

Notes

1 Many thanks to Gary Anderson, then Senior Economist within the Technology Partnerships Office at NIST, who graciously made these data available. Also see the Note to Figure 4.5.
2 The primary data included one customer from Alaska, one customer from Hawaii, and five customers from Puerto Rico.
3 NIST also has a research facility in Boulder, CO. See www.nist.gov/director/pao/nist-boulder-laboratories-precision-measurements-support-innovation (accessed December 7, 2020). Only the Gaithersburg, MD location was considered.
4 The cost for calibration services is variable depending on the calibration test required. See www.nist.gov/nvlap/nvlap-fee-structure (accessed December 14, 2020).
5 The NETS database was created and is managed by Walls & Associates. It was developed from the Duns Marketing Information (DMI) file that considers over 34 million establishments beginning in 1990. For a description of the database see www.kauffman.org/entrepreneurship/research/data-resources/ (accessed December 14, 2020).
6 Other industrial groupings were not considered.

6 Summary remarks and a roadmap for possible future research

As discussed in the previous chapters, the economics of metrology is an important topic in economics that has often been overlooked by researchers from a number of fields. There are notable benefits associated with the promulgation of and adoption of measurement standards. These benefits are not only grounded in the economic theory of information asymmetries and transaction costs, but also through empirical studies that have found a strong positive relationship between public sector investments in measurement standards and economic performance.

There is an area of study in which the economics of metrology belongs but has long been overlooked, and that area relates to the intersection of technology policy and innovation policy and measurement standards activities.

Consider the following two definitions. Technology policy is policy to enhance the application of new knowledge to some known problem. Innovation policy is policy to enhance the commercialization of a new technology in the market. Generally speaking, technology policy focuses on incentives to expand investments in R&D, and innovation policy focuses on lessening barriers for firms and organizations to introduce successfully new technology into the market.

Many countries have adopted mechanisms to enhance private sector investments in R&D. These incentives fall within three broadly defined areas. One area relates to incentives for private sector firms to invest more, another area relates to direct public sector support of R&D, and the third area relates to changes in the R&D environment faced by private sector firms.

Tax incentives are a form of the former, research grants are a form of direct support, and relaxed constraints for collaborative R&D are a form of a changed R&D environment. In the United States, the research and experimentation (R&E) tax credit of 1981 is the primary tax incentive available to firms (that can benefit from a tax credit). The Small Business

DOI: 10.4324/9781003186953-6

Innovation Research (SBIR) program established in 1982 is an example of public sector support to small firms to undertake new R&D projects. And, the National Cooperative Research Act of 1984 is an example of how relaxed antitrust guidelines have incentivized firms to collaborate on R&D.

> *To date, there has not been serious highest-level policy discussions about the nexus between enhanced measurement standards and the effectiveness of the technology policies just described* [emphasis added].[1]

There have certainly been academic and policy discussions about the role of enhanced measurement standards. For example, Tassey wrote (2020, p. 304):

> High-tech infrastructure, such as data on materials properties, machine calibration techniques, functional (as opposed to physical) interfaces among components of technologically advanced product and information systems, and product testing algorithms to assure buyers of performance, permeate technology-based manufacturing supply chains at all stages of economic activity.

And, Tassey's statement here parallels the discussion in the previous chapters of this book.

There have also been academic and policy discussions about new technology policy efforts. For example, in the United States a bill to establish a new Directorate for Technology in a redesigned National Science Foundation was recently introduced in the U.S. Senate as S. 3832; it is called the Endless Frontier Act in honour of the 1945 report by Dr. Vannevar Bush, *Science—the Endless Frontier*.[2,3] If made into law, the act would legislate:

> a significant increase in investment in research, education, technology transfer, and the core strengths of the United States innovation ecosystem. [Without such] it is only a matter of time before the global competitors of the United States overtake the United States in terms of technological primacy.

However, nowhere in the bill is there a detailed discussion of how the capabilities at NIST might leverage the "increase in investment in research, education, technology transfer, and the core strengths of the United States innovation ecosystem."

Consider Figure 6.1. The figure should be viewed as one method to envisage the importance of the emphasized statement in italics offered above. Measured on the horizontal level is the level of investment in R&D by a private sector firm. Measured on the vertical axis is the rate of return to an investment in R&D by a private sector firm. The firm faces a downward slowing marginal rate of return schedule due to diminishing returns to investments in R&D. Given the firm's assumed to be constant marginal private cost of conducting R&D, which is conceptualized in percentage terms as the opportunity cost of R&D investments (e.g., x%), the optimal level of investment in R&D for this firm is at the level RD_0. With enhanced measurement standards, it is assumed that the firm's marginal rate of return schedule will increase, as shown by a rightward shift in its marginal rate of return schedule to the marginal rate of return schedule so labelled to reflect enhanced measurement standards.[4]

Given an initial level of R&D investment of RD_0 and given the new marginal rate of return schedule with enhanced measurement standards, the firm's marginal private cost at an R&D investment of RD_0 will be less than its marginal private rate of return from an R&D investment of RD_0. The firm will maximize profits by increasing its R&D investment from RD_0 to RD_1, where its marginal rate of return with enhanced measurement standards from an R&D investment of RD_1 equals the firm's marginal private cost from an R&D investment in the same amount. Enhanced measurement standards *per se* will increase private sector R&D investments under the

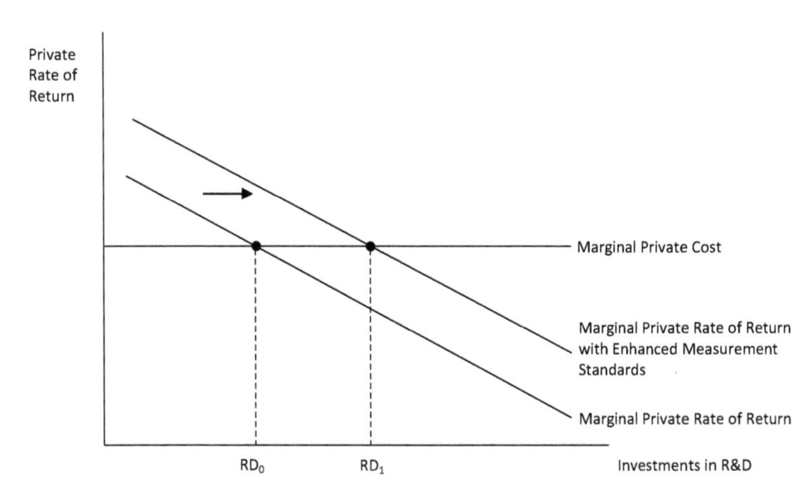

Figure 6.1 The implication of improved measurement standards for an R&D-based firm

stated assumptions,[5] but when done in relationship to technology policies the leveraging effect could be even greater.

How does one study in a systematic manner the implications from Figure 6.1?

One micro approach might involve series of case studies of private sector firms that have benefitted from, for example, an R&E tax credit or had received an SBIR award. With a complete understanding of the technology resulting from the additional investments in R&D, one could within an accepted evaluation methodology (Link and Scott, 2012, 2019), develop counterfactual interview questions about the outcomes from hypothetical measurement standards existing.

One macro approach might involve enhanced time series data from a nation's metrology laboratory that quantifies metrics related to advancements in measurement standards so that one could engage events studies using aggregate performance measures.

As researchers pursue topics related to the economics of metrology in the future, they might keep in mind the wisdom attributed to Alfred Nobel: "If I have a thousand ideas and only one turns out to be good, I am satisfied."[6]

Notes

1 This statement is emphasized with no intention of valorizing this proposition, but rather it is emphasized in an effort to initiate additional research on this topic.

2 See www.congress.gov/bill/116th-congress/senate-bill/3832/text (accessed December 18, 2020).

3 On November 17, 1944, U.S. President Franklin D. Roosevelt sent a letter to Dr. Vannevar Bush, then Director of the Office of Scientific Research and Development. The letter requested Dr. Bush to, among other things, address the question: what can the Government do now and in the future to aid research activities by public and private organizations? On July 5, 1945, Dr. Bush sent his report, *Science—the Endless Frontier*, to President Harry S. Truman (President Roosevelt passed on April 12, 1945) setting forth an agenda along with the seeds for what eventually became the National Science Foundation.

4 The adoption of a new measurement standard may be more costly to use and thus the marginal private rate of return schedule with the enhanced measurement standard may shift to the left. The new equilibrium level of R&D might then be less than RD_0. However, it may be the case that the new investment level of R&D may create greater value. I thank John Scott for pointing out that this case may be illustrated using a construct developed in Kohn and Scott (1982). One might think of a downward sloping marginal cost of R&D schedule (R&D per unit of R&D output) and an upward sloping marginal value curve from a greater R&D output. In such a model, the adoption of an enhanced measurement standard may increase the marginal value of R&D schedule to the right thus yielding a greater level of equilibrium R&D output.

5 All of the studies referenced in Table 2.1 were conducted holding technology policy constant. The noted economic outcomes of the measurement standards under study would be greater if there were, for an example, a concomitant or attendant technology policy to increase R&D investments.

6 See www.goodreads.com/quotes/671953-if-i-have-a-thousand-ideas-and-only-one-turns (accessed December 18, 2020).

References

Akerlof, George A. (1970). "The Market for 'Lemons': Quality Uncertainty and the Market Mechanism," *Quarterly Journal of Economics*, 84: 488–500.

Allen, Douglas W. (1999). "Transaction Costs," in *Encyclopedia of Law & Economics*, https://reference.findlaw.com/lawandeconomics/literature-reviews/0740-transaction-costs.html (accessed November 7, 2020).

Audretsch, David B., Dennis Patrick Leyden, and Albert N. Link (2012). "Universities as Research Partners in Publicly Supported Entrepreneurial Firms," *Economics of Innovation and New Technology*, 21: 529–545.

Barzel, Yoram (1982). "Measurement Cost and the Organization of Markets," *Journal of Law & Economics*, 25: 27–48.

Bator, Francis M. (1958). "The Anatomy of Market Failure," *Quarterly Journal of Economics*, 72: 351–379.

Birch, John (2003). *Benefit of Legal Metrology for the Economy and Society*, report prepared for the International Committee of Legal Metrology, Australia.

Blind, Knut, Andre Jungmittag, and Axel Mangelsdorf (2011). *The Economic Benefits of Standardization: An Update of the Study Carried Out by DIN in 2000*, Berlin: DIN German Institute for Standardization.

Blind, Knut, Kakob Pohlisch, and Anne Rainville (2020). "Innovation and Standardization as Drivers of Companies' Success in Public Procurement: An Empirical Analysis," *Journal of Technology Transfer*, 45: 664–693.

Choudhary, M. Ali, P. T., and L. Zhao (2013). "Taking the Measure of Things: The Role of Measurement in EU Trade," *Empirica*, 40: 75–109.

Cochrane, Rexmond H. (1966). *Measures for Progress: A History of the National Bureau of Standards*, Washington, DC: National Bureau of Standards.

Commons, John R. (1931). "Institutional Economics," *American Economic Review*, 21: 648–657.

David, Paul A. and Shane Greenstein (1990). "The Economics of Compatibility Standards: An Introduction to Recent Research," *Economics of Innovation and New Technology*, 1: 3–41.

De Simone, Daniel V. and Charles F. Treat (1971). *A History of the Metric System Controversy in the United States*, Gaithersburg, MD: National Institute of Standards and Technology.

Department of Business, Energy & Industrial Strategy (2017). *UK Measurement Strategy: Confidence in Investment, Trade and Innovation*, London: U.K. Department of Business, Energy & Industrial Strategy.

DTI (2005). *The Empirical Economics of Standards*, DTI Economics Monograph 12, London: U.K. Department of Industry and Trade.

Filho, Bruno A. Rodrigues and Rodrigo F. Gonçalves (2015). "Legal Metrology, the Economy and Society: A Systematic Literature Review," *Measurement*, 69: 155–163.

Foucart, Renaud and Qian Cher Li (2021). "The Role of Technology Standards in Product Innovation: Theory and Evidence from UK Manufacturing Firms," *Research Policy*, 50: 104157.

Frazier, Arthur H. (1978). *United States Standards of Weights and Measures: Their Creation and Creators*, Washington, DC: Smithsonian Institution Press.

Hall, Bronwyn H., Jacques Mairesse, and Pierre Mohnen (2010). "Measuring the Returns to R&D," in *Economics of Innovation*, B. Hall and N. Rosenberg, eds., pp. 1033–1082, Amsterdam: Elsevier.

Harris, William T. and Lydia Harris (1996). "The Political Economy of Metrology," *Humanity and Society*, 20: 70–77.

Himbert, Marc E. (2009). "A Brief History of Measurement," *The European Physical Journal, Special Topics*, 172: 25–35.

International Trade Centre (2004). *Legal Metrology and International Trade*, Geneva: International Trade Centre.

Judson, Lewis V. (1976). *Weights and Measures Standards of the United States: A Brief History*, Washington, DC: National Bureau of Standards.

Jula, Payman (2001). "The Economic Impact of Metrology Methods in Semiconductor Manufacturing," University of California, Berkeley Technical Report No. UCB/ERL M01/22.

Kaarls, Robert (2007). "Metrology, Essential to Trade, Industry and Society," *Accreditation and Quality Assurance*, 12: 435–437.

King, Michael, Ray Lambert, and Paul Temple (2017). "Measurement Standards and Productivity Spillovers," in *Handbook of Innovation and Standards*, R. Hawkins, K. Blind, and R. Page, eds., pp. 162–186, Cheltenham, UK: Edward Elgar Publishing.

Klaes, Matthias (2000). "The History of the Concept of Transaction Costs: Neglected Aspects," *Journal of the History of Economic Thought*, 22: 191–216.

Kohn, Meir and John T. Scott (1982). "Scale Economies in Research and Development: The Schumpeterian Hypothesis," *Journal of Industrial Economics*, 30: 239–249.

Lambert, Ray (2010). "Economic Impact of the National Measurement System," Report for the National Measurement Office, UK.

Leech, David P. and John T. Scott (2011). *The Economic Impacts of Documentary Standards: A Case Study of the Flat Panel Display Measurement Standard (FPDM)*, Gaithersburg, MD: National Institute of Standards and Technology.

Leyden, Dennis Patrick and Albert N. Link (2015). *Public Sector Entrepreneurship: U.S. Technology and Innovation Policy*, New York: Oxford University Press.

Link, Albert N. (1983). "Market Structure and Voluntary Product Standards," *Applied Economics*, 15: 393–401.

Link, Albert N. (1996). *Evaluating Public Sector Research and Development*, New York: Praeger.

Link, Albert N. (2019). "Technology Transfer at the US National Institute of Standards and Technology," *Science and Public Policy*, 46: 906–912.

Link, Albert N. (2021). "The Economics of Metrology: An Exploratory Study of the Impact of Measurement Science on U.S. Productivity," *Economics of Innovation and New Technology*, DOI: 10.1080/10438599.2021.1895905.

Link, Albert N. and Zachary T. Oliver (2000). *Technology Transfer and US Public Sector Innovation*, New York: Edward Elgar.

Link, Albert N. and John T. Scott (1998). *Public Accountability: Evaluating Technology-Based Institutions*, Boston: Kluwer Academic Publishers.

Link, Albert N. and John T. Scott (2011). *Public Goods, Public Gains: Calculating the Social Benefits of Public R&D*, New York: Oxford University Press.

Link, Albert N. and John T. Scott (2012). *The Theory and Practice of Public-Sector R&D Economic Impact Analysis*, Gaithersburg, MD: National Institute of Standards and Technology.

Link, Albert N. and John T. Scott (2019). *The Social Value of New Technology*, New York: Edward Elgar.

Link, Albert N. and Donald S. Siegel (2003). *Technological Change and Economic Performance*. London: Routledge.

Marshall, Alfred (1920). *Industry and Trade*, London: Macmillan and Co.

Martin, Keith and Barbara P. Silcox (2010). *Responding to National Needs: Supplement to Appendices 1994–2009*, Gaithersburg, MD: National Institute of Standards and Technology.

Michell, Joel (2005). "The Logic of Measurement," *Measurement*, 38: 285–294.

National Physical Laboratory (2010). *A Beginners Guide to Measurement*, Good Practice Guide 118, UK.

Porter, Theodore M. (2001). "Economics and the History of Measurement," *History of Political Economy*, 33(Suppl-1): 4–22.

Research Triangle Institute (RTI) (2000). "Economic Impact of Standard Reference Materials for Sulfur in Fossil Fuels," NIST Planning Report 00-1, Gaithersburg, MD.

Richardson, Elliot L. (1976). "Brief History of Measurement Systems, with a Chart of the Modernized Metric System," *National Bureau of Standards Special Publication* 304A, Washington, DC: U.S. Department of Commerce.

Robertson, Kristel and Jan A. Swanepoel (2015). *The Economics of Metrology*, Canberra, ACT: Office of the Chief Economist, Department of Industry, Innovation and Science, Australian Government.

Savio, Enrico, Leonardo De Chiffre, Simone Carmignato, and Jørgen Meinertz (2016). "Economic Benefits of Metrology in Manufacturing," *CIRP Annals - Manufacturing Technology*, 65: 495–498.

Schooley, James F. (2000). *Responding to National Needs: The National Bureau of Standards Becomes the National Institute of Standards and Technology, 1969–1993*, Washington, DC: National Institute of Standards and Technology.

Scott, Troy J. and John T. Scott (2015). "Standards and Innovation: U.S. Public/Private Partnerships to Support Technology-based Economic Growth," *Economics of Innovation and New Technology*, 24: 457–489.

Seiler, Eberhard (1999). "The Role of Metrology in Economic and Social Development," *Computer Standards & Interfaces*, 21: 77–88.

Smith, Adam (1776, 1914). *An Inquiry into the Nature and Causes of the Wealth of Nations*, London: J.M Dent & Sons.

Spencer, Christopher and Paul Temple (2016). "Standards, Learning, and Growth in Britain, 1901–2009," *Economic History Review*, 69: 627–652.

Stokes, Fiona, Hugh Dixon, Amapola Generosa, and Ganesh Nana (2011). *The Economic Benefits of Standards to New Zealand*, Wellington: The Standards Council of New Zealand and The Building Research Association of New Zealand.

Swann, G. M. Peter (2009). "The Economics of Metrology and Measurement," Report for National Measurement Office, Department for Business, Innovation and Skills, London UK.

Swann, G. M. Peter (2010). "The Economics of Standardization: An Update," Report for the Department for Business, Innovation and Skills, London, UK.

TASC (2000). "Economic Impact Assessment: NIST-EEEL Laser and Fiberoptic Power and Energy Calibration Services," NIST Planning Report 00-3, Gaithersburg, MD.

Tassey, Gregory (1982). "Infratechnologies and the Role of Government," *Technological Forecasting and Social Change*, 21: 163–180.

Tassey, Gregory (2010). "Rationales and Mechanisms for Revitalizing US Manufacturing R&D Strategies," *Journal of Technology Transfer*, 35: 283–333.

Tassey, Gregory (2017). "The Roles and Impacts of Technical Standards on Economic Growth and Implications for Innovation Policy," *Annals of Science and Technology Policy*, 1: 215–316.

Temple, Paul and Geoffrey Williams (2002). "Infra-technology and Economic Performance: Evidence from the United Kingdom Measurement Infrastructure," *Information Economics and Policy*, 14: 435–452.

U.S. Department of Commerce (USDOC) (1990). *Emerging Technologies: A Survey of Technical and Economic Opportunities*, Washington, DC: U.S. Department of Commerce.

U.S. Department of Commerce (USDOC) (2019). *Annual Report on Technology Transfer: Approach and Plans, Fiscal Year 2019 Activities and Achievements*, U.S. Department of Commerce, Gaithersburg, MD: National Institute of Standards and Technology.

Williamson, Oliver E. (1979). "Transaction Cost Economics: The Governance of Contractual Relations," *Journal of Law and Economics*, 22: 233–261.

Index